THE CURRY KITCHEN

★ ★

Classic, Spicy & Satisfying

150

GREAT RECIPES

★

CONTENTS

Introduction 4

Poultry ● 7

Meat ● 57

Seafood and Fish ● 109

Beans and Pulses ● 141

Vegetables ● 171

Bread, Condiments and Rice ● 221

Index 254

INTRODUCTION

With 150 curry recipes in this book, there's certain to be something for everyone. We've got the basics covered: if you need the best recipe for butter chicken, a good dahl or Thai green curry, you'll find it here. But we've straddled the globe to uncover some less well-known curries too. Why not try your hand at something new – bobotie or doro wat from Africa perhaps – or cook up a stack of spicy Jamaican beef patties next time you have friends over.

As we were preparing the recipes for this book, we got to thinking 'What is curry anyway?' Here's an interesting fact: the word 'curry' was introduced by British colonialists in India in the 18th century. It's thought to be a corruption of the Tamil word 'kari', meaning sauce. Indians had been cooking with tamarind, onion, coriander, chilli pepper, turmeric, cumin, fenugreek, pepper and mustard long before the British decided to call it curry, but some clarification must have been required because in 1889 at the Paris Universal Exposition a formal curry decree established the prescribed quantities of each ingredient.

Things have relaxed a bit since then, and pretty much anything and everything can be curried. In this book, we've got curried sausages and chips, curried eggs benedict (an idea for breakfast perhaps), fruit-based curries such as pineapple, mango and jackfruit, curry pie and even a curry salad. While the word 'curry' might have originally referred to the sauce or gravy, 'curried' nowadays might best be defined as any food that contains spice - in some way, shape or form.

Curries are most commonly found in the cuisines of India, Pakistan, Bangladesh, Sri Lanka, Nepal, Indonesia, Malaysia, Thailand, Vietnam and the Caribbean. All of those cuisines are represented in this book, including some classics like laksa and nasi lemak that you'll definitely be familiar with from your local Indonesian restaurant. Why not try it at home? We've also included curries from Africa, South and Central America and Japan, if you feel like expanding your curry cooking skills and knowledge.

Curry is becoming a staple on dining tables across the world. But how do you make an excellent curry? You'll learn how from the recipes in this book, but here's a tip: don't neglect your onions. Many curry recipes start with the simple frying of an onion. If you want a light curry, fry your onion until pale and soft. For a rich, dark curry fry your onion for longer, until it's gooey and caramelised. Also, be generous with spices. Curry is all about bold flavours, so don't be shy. The last element of your curry to consider is the gravy. Is it milky and coconut-based, saucey and tomato-based or sticky and onion-based? You decide.

For ease of use, the recipes in this book have been broken down into the following sections: poultry; beef, lamb and pork; fish and seafood; vegetarian; and accompaniments. There's something in here for every member of the family, from the curry sceptic through to the chilli-muncher in your household. If you're looking for mild or spicy, healthy or decadent, meat-based or vegetarian, you'll find a recipe in this book to enjoy and come back to time and again.

Making curry is easy, and it's for everyone. With this book, cooks can perfect the familiar recipes and experiment with the unknown. So, crack open the spice cupboard and get sizzling those onions. Enjoy!

POULTRY

Easy red chicken curry   8
Hot Japanese ramen   10
Spicy chicken breast   12
Chicken coconut curry   13
Jerk chicken   14
Spicy Korean chicken   16
Chicken tikka wrap   18
Chicken vindaloo   19
Burmese curry noodles   20
The best butter chicken   22
Sweet duck red curry   24
Chicken massaman curry   25
Chicken malvani   26
Tandoori chicken kebabs with raita   28
Korean fire chicken   30
Curried chicken salad   31
Chicken tikka masala   32
Chicken haleem   34
Classic chicken curry   36
Sweet chicken curry pie   37
Chicken laksa   38
Spicy okra and chicken gumbo   40
Bombay chicken wings   42
Balti chicken   43
Charred tandoori drumsticks   44
Green chicken curry   46
Easy tandoori chicken   48
Chicken and potato curry   49
Chicken jalfrezi   50
Doro wat (Ethiopian curry)   52
Chicken noodle khao soi   54

EASY RED CHICKEN CURRY

INGREDIENTS

1½ tbsps Thai red curry paste

8 chicken thigh fillets, cubed

1½ tbsps vegetable oil

1 x 400ml (14fl oz) can coconut milk

2 tbsps fish sauce

3 tsps brown sugar

2 large dried chillies, roughly chopped

250g (8oz) green beans, trimmed and sliced (optional)

Coriander leaves and red chillies, to garnish

METHOD

1. Put the chicken and curry paste in a mixing bowl, and toss to coat. Cover the bowl and if time allows place in the fridge for 1 hour.

2. Heat oil in a wok over medium heat. Fry the chicken for 2 to 3 minutes or until lightly browned. Pour in the coconut milk and reduce heat to a low simmer. Cook, stirring occasionally, for 5 minutes or until chicken is tender.

3. Stir in fish sauce and sugar. Cook for a further minute. Add chillies and beans, if using. Cook for 3 to 4 minutes or until beans are tender.

4. Serve in bowls with curry laddled over jasmine or basmati rice and topped with chopped coriander and whole chillies.

HOT JAPANESE RAMEN

INGREDIENTS

2 chicken breasts

Salt and pepper,
to season

1 tbsp butter

2 tsps sesame or
vegetable oil

2 tsps fresh ginger,
minced

3 tsps fresh garlic,
minced

3 tbsps soy sauce

2 tbsps mirin

4 cups (1L, 2pt) rich
chicken stock

½ tsp chilli powder

25g (1oz) dried shitake
mushrooms (optional)

1 tsp salt

2 eggs

180g (6oz) ramen
noodles (dried or fresh)

½ cup (50g, 2oz)
spring onions, sliced

½ cup (50g, 2oz)
bean sprouts

METHOD

1. Preheat the oven to 190°C (375°F, Gas Mark 5). Season the chicken generously with salt and pepper. Melt the butter in a large oven-safe frying pan. Add the chicken, skin-side down, and fry for 5-6 minutes or until golden brown. Flip and fry a further 4-5 minutes, until golden. Transfer the pan to the oven and roast for 15-20 minutes, until the chicken is cooked through. Remove from the oven, transfer the chicken to a plate and cover with foil until ready to serve.

2. Heat the oil in a large pot over medium heat, until shimmering. Add the garlic and ginger, and cook until softened. Add the soy sauce and mirin, and stir to combine. Cook for another minute. Add the stock and chilli powder, cover, and bring to boil. Remove the lid and let simmer uncovered for 5 minutes, then add the mushrooms, if using. Simmer gently for another 10 minutes, and season with salt, to taste.

3. Fill a pot with sufficient water to cover the eggs, and bring to a boil. Gently lower the eggs into the boiling water, and simmer for 7 minutes. Retain the boiling water. Remove eggs and rinse in cold water. When cool enough to handle, peel away the shells and slice in half.

4. Add the ramen noodles to the boiling water. Cook for 2-3 minutes, until soft, then divide the noodles into two large bowls. Slice the chicken and add to the bowl. Garnish with fresh green onions, bean sprouts and soft boiled egg. Serve immediately.

SPICY CHICKEN BREAST

INGREDIENTS

¼ cup (40g, 1½ oz) brown sugar

3 tbsps paprika

2 tsps cumin

1 tbsp garlic, minced

1 tsp salt

¼ tsp pepper

4 boneless, skinless chicken breasts

METHOD

1. Preheat oven to 215°C (420°F, Gas Mark 7).

2. Place brown sugar, paprika, cumin, garlic, and salt and pepper into a plastic bag and shake to combine.

3. Add chicken breasts and seal or hold the bag tight. Shake again to coat chicken.

4. Transfer chicken to a bowl and cover. Leave to marinade in the fridge for 1-3 hours, or overnight, to absorb the flavours.

5. Arrange chicken breasts on a lined baking tray. Transfer to the oven and bake for 25 minutes.

CHICKEN COCONUT CURRY

INGREDIENTS

1 tbsp vegetable oil

1 onion, finely chopped

3 garlic cloves, finely chopped

1 tsp ground turmeric

2 tbsps yellow curry paste

6 boneless chicken thigh fillets, cut into pieces

1 x 400ml (14fl oz) can coconut milk

1-2 tsps fish sauce, to taste

Juice of 1 lime, plus wedges to serve

Sprig of mint or Thai basil, and sliced chilli, to serve

METHOD

1. Heat oil in a large saucepan over medium heat. Add the onion and cook for 5-7 minutes until softened. Stir in the garlic, tumeric and curry paste and cook for 1 minute until fragrant. Add chicken to the pan stirring to coat in paste, and cook for 2-3 minutes.

2. Pour in the coconut milk and stir. Bring to the boil, then reduce heat to medium-low and simmer, stirring occasionally, for 15 minutes until chicken is almost cooked. Add fish sauce and lime juice to taste.

3. Serve in bowls on top of rice and with a garnish of mint and sliced chilli.

JERK CHICKEN

INGREDIENTS

Marinade

3 spring onions, chopped

4 garlic cloves, chopped

1 onion, chopped

3 habanero chillies, seeded

¼ cup (60ml, 2fl oz) fresh lime juice

2 tbsps soy sauce

3 tbsps olive oil

1 tbsps salt

1 tbsp brown sugar

1 tbsp fresh or dried thyme

2 tsps ground allspice

1 tsp pepper

1 tsp ground nutmeg

½ tsp cinnamon

Chicken

16 chicken drumsticks

Lime wedges, to serve

METHOD

1. Place marinade ingredients in blender and process until smooth.

2. Place chicken and marinade in a large bowl or sealable plastic bags. Rub marinade into chicken with your hands and cover bowl or press excess air from bags, seal, then turn over several times to distribute marinade. Transfer to fridge and chill for 24 hours, turning once or twice.

3. Remove chicken from fridge 1 hour before cooking and place in a heatproof dish.

4. Preheat burners of gas grill to high. Adjust heat to moderate before placing chicken underneath. Cook for 15 minutes or until well browned on all sides. Adjust heat to low and cook chicken for 15 minutes until cooked through.

SPICY KOREAN CHICKEN

INGREDIENTS

350g (12oz) Korean
glass noodles

6 boneless chicken thigh
fillets, cut into pieces

6 dried red chillies

⅔ cup (160ml, 5fl oz)
soy sauce

2 tbsps oyster sauce

1 cup (250ml, 8fl oz)
water

3 cloves garlic, minced

2 tsps ginger, minced

4 tbsps brown sugar

1 tsp pepper

1 onion, sliced

2 carrots, sliced

1 small eggplant,
finely diced

2-3 zucchini, sliced

1 fresh red chilli, sliced

3 spring onions,
sliced, to serve

1 tbsp sesame seeds,
to serve

METHOD

1. Soak the noodles in warm water and set aside until ready
    to use.

2. Place chicken in a pot over medium-high heat and pour in
    enough water to cover the chicken. Bring to the boil and cook
    for 3 minutes. Remove the chicken and discard the water.
    Return the chicken to the pot and add the dried chillies.

3. In a bowl, combine soy sauce, oyster sauce, water, garlic, ginger,
    sugar and pepper. Pour mixture over the chicken and chillies.

4. Bring the mixture to a gentle boil and cover the pot. Simmer
    over medium-low heat for 20 minutes.

5. Add the onion, carrots and eggplant to the pot and simmer
    for a further 10 minutes.

6. Add the zucchini and chilli, and cook for 5 minutes or until
    tender, with the pan half covered.

7. Drain the noodles from the soaking water and add to the pot.
    Continue to cook, uncovered, for 3-5 minutes, until the noodles
    are tender yet still have bite.

8. Remove the pot from the heat and serve garnished with spring
    onion and sesame seeds.

CHICKEN TIKKA WRAP

INGREDIENTS

2 chicken breast fillets, cubed

1 tbsp tikka masala paste

2½ cups (625ml, 20fl oz) yoghurt

Oil, for frying

1 onion, chopped

1 cucumber, seeded and chopped

¹/₃ cup (15g, ½ oz) fresh mint, chopped

1 red onion, chopped

4 pita breads

Iceberg lettuce, to serve

METHOD

1. Place paste and 2 tablespoons yoghurt in a bowl and stir. Add chicken and mix through.

2. Heat oil in a small frying pan on a medium-high heat. Add onion and fry for 5 minutes or until soft and translucent. Set aside.

3. Cook chicken on a heated lightly oiled chargrill plate (or barbecue) for 10 minutes or until browned all over and cooked thorough. Rest for 5 min, before slicing thinly.

3. Mix together cucumber, mint, onion and remaining yoghurt in a medium sized bowl.

4. To serve, spread yoghurt mix over each piece of pita bread, top with chicken and onion and roll to enclose filling. Serve with lettuce.

CHICKEN VINDALOO

INGREDIENTS

3 chicken breasts, diced

Marinade

½ tsp lemon juice

2 tbsps white wine vinegar

1 onion, finely chopped

3 cloves garlic, finely minced

Medium piece ginger, finely minced

1 tsp garam masala powder

1 tsp ground cumin

1 tsp ground coriander

1 tsp cayenne pepper

½ tsp brown mustard seeds

4 tbsp vegetable oil

Curry

Oil, for frying

1 onion, finely chopped

½ tsp cinnamon

½ tsp chilli pepper

½ tsp cayenne pepper

½ tsp salt

Coriander leaves, to garnish

METHOD

1. In a large bowl, combine the marinade ingredients and mix thoroughly. Add the chicken and ensure it is well coated with the marinade. Cover and refrigerate for 3-4 hours, or longer if possible.

2. Heat oil in a large frying pan over a medium-high heat. Add the spices and onion and cook, stirring constantly, for 5-7 minutes or until onion is golden brown but not burnt.

3. Add the chicken mixture and cook, stirring frequently, for 5 minutes on medium-high heat.

4. Reduce heat cover and simmer for 20 minutes until the chicken is cooked through.

5. Garnish with fresh coriander to serve.

BURMESE CURRY NOODLES

INGREDIENTS

1 tbsp oil

Small piece ginger, finely chopped

4 garlic cloves, chopped

1 onion, chopped

3 boneless chicken thighs, diced

1 tsp red chilli flakes

½ tsp turmeric

½ tsp garam masala powder

1 tsp Thai red curry paste

2 cups (500ml, 1pt) chicken stock

1 tbsp fish sauce (optional)

1 tbsp besan (chickpea flour or gram flour)

2 spring onions, sliced, and coriander leaves, chopped, to garnish

125g (4oz) udon noodles, cooked according to instructions on the packet

METHOD

1. Heat oil in a frying pan over medium-high heat. Add ginger and garlic and fry for 1 minute, then add onions and fry for approximately 5 minutes or until golden brown.

2. Add chicken, chilli flakes, turmeric, garam masala and curry paste and stir to combine. Add chicken stock, salt to taste and fish sauce, if using. Mix everything together and bring to a boil, before reducing heat to a gentle simmer.

3. Combine besan and water to make a paste and pour in to the curry while stirring. Cook for 20 minutes or until chicken is cooked through. Before serving stir in spring onions and coriander and cook for 2 minutes.

4. Serve in a bowl on top of noodles.

THE BEST BUTTER CHICKEN

INGREDIENTS

4 boneless, skinless
chicken breasts, cubed

Marinade

2 tbsps lemon juice

2 cloves garlic, minced

1 tbsp garam masala

1 tsp salt

Curry

¼ cup (60ml, 2fl oz)
vegetable oil

2 onions, coarsely chopped

2 tbsps garlic, coarsely
chopped

2 tbsps garam masala

2 tsp paprika

¼ tsp cinnamon

2 tsp salt, or to taste

1 x 400 g (20oz)
can diced tomatoes

¾ cup (185ml, 6fl oz)
heavy cream

2 tbsps butter

Mint sprigs, to garnish

METHOD

1. Combine all marinade ingredients with the chicken in a flat-bottomed dish, rubbing the marinade into the chicken. Stand at room temperature while you prepare the sauce, or place in the fridge to marinate for 3-4 hours or overnight.

2. Heat oil over medium heat in a large saucepan. Add onions and cook slowly until golden, about 20 minutes, reducing heat if they are starting to burn.

3. Add garlic and cook until fragrant, about 1 minute. Stir in garam masala, paprika, cinnamon and salt and cook. After 1 minute, add tomatoes and cook for a further 2 minutes. Stir in the cream and then puree using an immersion blender if you have one. If using a standing blender, puree in batches.

4. Return sauce to pan and bring to a simmer. Add chicken, cover, and continue to simmer gently over medium-low heat until cooked through, about 10 minutes.

5. Stir in butter, and add salt to taste. Serve sprinkled with mint, if desired.

SWEET DUCK RED CURRY

INGREDIENTS

1⅓ cups (330ml, 11fl oz)
coconut cream

1½ tbsps red curry paste

3 tbsps Thai fish sauce

1 tbsp palm sugar

2 kaffir lime leaves,
torn into pieces

200g (7oz) roast duck,
thinly sliced

1 Thai eggplant, sliced

2¼ cups (560ml, 18fl oz)
coconut milk

6 lychees, peeled

6 small cherry tomatoes

½ small pineapple,
cut into pieces

Sweet basil leaves,
to garnish

2 tbsps coconut cream,
to garnish

METHOD

1. Pour the coconut cream into a wok or saucepan and bring to the boil before reducing the heat and simmering for 2 minutes, stirring constantly, until the coconut oil begins to separate out.

2. Stir in the curry paste, fish sauce, palm sugar and torn kaffir lime leaves. Simmer for 2 more minutes.

3. Add the duck and eggplant. Bring to a boil. Then add the coconut milk and simmer for 5 minutes.

4. Add the lychees and cherry tomatoes and simmer for 2 minutes. Then add the pineapple. Turn off the heat and serve garnished with the sweet basil and coconut cream.

CHICKEN MASSAMAN CURRY

INGREDIENTS

2 tbsp vegetable oil

2 onions, sliced

2 chicken breasts, cut into large pieces

3 tbsps massaman curry paste

2 potatoes, cut into chunks

2 bird's-eye chillies, halved lengthways

2 cups (500ml, 1pt) chicken stock

¾ cup (200ml, 7fl oz) coconut milk

2 tomatoes, roughly chopped

2 tbsps fish sauce

1½ tbsps palm sugar

2 tbsps soy sauce

1 lime, juiced

2 tbsps peanut butter

25g (1oz) roasted peanuts, roughly chopped

METHOD

1. Heat the oil in a large saucepan or casserole over a medium heat. Add the onions and fry for 8-10 minutes, or until softened and golden-brown. Remove onions from pan and set aside.

2. Increase to a high heat then add the chicken and fry for 2-3 minutes, turning constantly, to ensure it is sealed all over.

3. Return onions to the pan. Add half of the massaman curry paste and stir well to coat the chicken and onions in the paste. Fry the mixture for 1-2 minutes, or until fragrant.

4. Add potato, chillies, chicken stock, coconut milk, tomatoes, fish sauce, palm sugar and soy sauce to the pan and stir well. Bring the curry to the boil, then cover and reduce heat to a simmer. Add the chicken and continue to simmer for 20 minutes, or until the chicken is cooked through but not dry.

5. Taste and season with fish sauce or lime juice as required. Before serving, stir in the peanut butter and peanuts.

CHICKEN MALVANI

INGREDIENTS

500g (1lb) chicken pieces

Marinade

Small piece ginger, sliced

5 garlic cloves, peeled

2 tbsps lemon juice

4 green chillies

½ bunch coriander
(retaining some for garnish)

1 tsp nutmeg powder

2 tsps salt

Curry

Oil, for frying

1 tsp caraway seeds

1 cinnamon stick

2 cardamom pods,
crushed

5-8 peppercorns

1 star anise

3 onions, chopped

1 cup (90g, 3oz) coconut,
grated

1 bay leaf

2 tbsps ginger-garlic paste

1 tsp red chilli powder

1 tbsp ground coriander

1 tbsp garam masala

Salt, to taste

METHOD

1. Finely chop and combine the ingredients for the marinade in a large bowl. Add the chicken and rub the marinade into it. Cover and refridgerate for 1 hour.

2. Heat 2 tablespoons oil in a wok or deep frying pan. When shimmering, add caraway seeds, cinnamon, cardamom, peppercorns and star anise. Cook for 1-2 minutes. Add half of the onions to the oil and fry for 3-4 minutes. Then add the grated coconut in the pan. Cook on low for a further 3 to 4 minutes until browned. Remove from heat and allow to cool.

3. Take the cooled mixture and grind into a paste using a food processor or pestle and mortar.

4. Heat oil in a pan at a medium-high heat until shimmering and add the bay leaf. Then add remaining onions and fry for 5 minutes or until golden. Add the ginger-garlic paste and cook on low for 2-3 minutes.

5. Add the marinated chicken to the pan and cook, stirring, on a medium heat for 3-4 minutes. Add salt, chilli powder, ground coriander and garam masala. Cook for a further 2-3 minutes.

6. Add the ground coconut and onion paste into the pan. Stir well to combine and then simmer for 5 minutes or until oil starts to separate.

7. Add 2 cups (500ml, 1pt) of water. Cover and cook on low heat for 7-10 minutes or until chicken is tender.

8. Garnish with a spoonful of plain yoghurt and coriander leaves.

TANDOORI CHICKEN KEBABS WITH RAITA

INGREDIENTS

¹/₃ cup (80ml, 3fl oz) tandoori paste

1 tbsp lime juice

¹/₃ cup (80ml, 3fl oz) thick plain yoghurt

3 chicken breasts, cut into chunks

1 cup (250ml, 8fl oz) plain yoghurt

2 garlic cloves, crushed

1 Lebanese cucumber, grated

¼ cup (10g, ¼ oz) mint leaves, finely chopped

Salt and pepper

Chapatti bread, to serve

Iceberg lettuce, red onion, cucumber and coriander leaves, to serve

METHOD

1. Soak 12 bamboo skewers or use metal skewers.

2. Combine tandoori paste, lime juice and thick yoghurt in a bowl.

3. Thread chicken onto skewers. Place in large flat dish and spoon over tandoori mixture. Turn to ensure even coating.

4. Cover and refrigerate for at least 3 hours.

5. Prepare the raita by combining yoghurt, garlic, cucumber, mint and salt and pepper in a bowl. Cover and refrigerate.

6. Prepare salad by slicing cucumber, lettuce and red onion and chopping coriander.

7. Remove skewers from marinade and cook on an oiled barbecue or chargrill pan, turning and basting with marinade occasionally, for 10 minutes or until cooked through.

8. Serve with raita, warm chapatti and salad.

KOREAN FIRE CHICKEN

INGREDIENTS

8 chicken thighs, diced

Marinade

3 tbsps soy sauce

1 tsp pepper

2 tbsps honey

3 tbsps rice wine

1 spring onion,
finely sliced

2 tsps sesame oil

Fire sauce

2 bird's-eye chillies

1 tsp chilli powder

1 pear, peeled
and cored

2 spring onions, halved

4 cloves garlic, peeled

4 tbsps soy sauce

2 tsps hot mustard

1 tbsp rice wine vinegar

1 tbsp sesame oil

2 tbsps honey

Oil, for frying

Toasted sesame
seeds, to garnish

METHOD

1. Place the ingredients for the marinade in a bowl and stir to combine. Add the chicken and coat well with marinade. Cover and marinate in the fridge at least 3 hours.

2. Place ingredients for the fire sauce in the blender and process until well combined. Adjust liquids to achieve the desired consistency and taste of sauce. Set aside.

3. Remove chicken from the fridge 30 minutes before cooking.

4. Heat oil in a frying pan over high heat. Fry chicken, stirring often, for 5-7 minutes until browned. Drain off excess oil. Reduce heat to medium and pour in the sauce. Cook for a further 10 minutes until cooked through.

5. Arrange the chicken on a serving plate and garnish with toasted sesame seeds to serve.

CURRIED CHICKEN SALAD

INGREDIENTS

2 tbsps ginger, minced

2 garlic cloves, minced

1 tbsp Madras curry powder

½ tsp salt

¼ tsp pepper

2 tbsp olive oil

1 cup (250ml, 8fl oz) plain yoghurt

3 chicken breasts

1 small eggplant, cubed

½ cup (125ml, 4fl oz) vegetable oil

1 cos lettuce

10 cherry tomatoes, halved

¼ cup (30g, 1oz) pine nuts

METHOD

1. Combine the ginger, garlic, curry powder, salt and pepper, olive oil and yoghurt in a mixing bowl and add chicken pieces. Turn the chicken through the marinade and then cover and refridgerate for 3-4 hours or overnight.

2. Preheat the oven to 230°C (445°F, Gas Mark 8). In a bowl, toss the eggplant in the vegetable oil and sprinkle with salt and pepper. Spread the eggplant on a large baking sheet. Arrange the chicken on top of the vegetables. Roast for about 30 minutes, rotating the pan halfway through, until the eggplant is soft and the chicken is nearly cooked through.

3. Meanwhile, arrange the lettuce, cherry tomatoes and pine nuts on a platter.

4. Transfer the chicken and vegetables to the platter and serve.

CHICKEN TIKKA MASALA

INGREDIENTS

12 boneless chicken thigh fillets, cut into chunks

100g (3½ oz) plain yoghurt

4 tbsps tikka masala paste

Oil, for frying

1 onion, finely chopped

1 green chilli, seeded, finely chopped

3 garlic cloves, crushed

Medium piece ginger, finely grated

1 cup (250ml, 8fl oz) chicken stock

1 x 400g (14oz) can chopped tomatoes

2 tsps tomato paste

$1/3$ cup (100ml, 3fl oz) thickened cream

1 tbsp fresh lemon juice

Fresh coriander, to garnish

METHOD

1. Combine chicken, yoghurt and half the tikka masala paste in a bowl. Season with salt and pepper and stir to combine. Cover and place in the fridge for 3-4 hours or longer to marinate.

2. Heat oil in a saucepan over medium heat. Add onion, chilli, garlic and ginger and stir for 5 minutes or until golden. Add the remaining curry paste and cook, stirring, for 2 minutes, or until aromatic.

3. Add stock, tomatoes and tomato paste. Bring to the boil and then reduce heat to low. Simmer for 15 minutes or until sauce thickens slightly.

4. Heat oil in a large frying pan over medium heat. Sear chicken and cook for 5 minutes or until lightly browned. Add chicken to sauce and simmer for 15 minutes or until cooked through.

5. Add cream and lemon juice 5 minutes before serving and stir well to combine. Garnish with coriander and serve with basmati rice.

CHICKEN HALEEM

INGREDIENTS

200g (7oz) whole wheat

$^1/_3$ cup (60g, 2oz) yellow split lentils

Oil, for frying

3 onions, thinly sliced

1 tbsp ginger, minced

1 tbsp garlic, minced

1 tsp garam masala powder

2 tbsps red chilli powder

1½ tbsps ground coriander

1 tsp ground turmeric

Salt, to taste

2 chicken breasts, cubed

2 cups (500ml, 1pt) water

Fresh coriander leaves finely chopped, lemon wedges and crispy onions, to garnish

METHOD

1. Place wheat in a bowl and cover with cold water. Soak for 1 hour 30 minutes. When finished, rinse and then transfer grains to a saucepan. Cover with salted water and cook for 20 minutes until soft. Set aside.

2. Place lentils in a bowl and soak for 30 minutes. Rinse and then cook lentils in boiling water for 10 minutes or until soft. Set aside.

3. Heat oil in a frying pan over medium-high heat. Add the onion and fry, stirring, for 5 minutes until soft. Add ginger and garlic and cook, stirring, for a further 2 minutes then add garam masala powder, red chilli powder, coriander, turmeric and salt and stir to coat onion with spices.

4. Add chicken and cook for 3-4 minutes until browned. Reduce heat to low. Add the wheat grains to the chicken and stir to combine.

5. Place lentils in a food processor with water and process until a thick paste forms. Pour the lentil paste into the curry and mix well to combine. Cook for 30 minutes.

6. Before serving, garnish with fried onions, coriander leaves and lemon wedges.

CLASSIC CHICKEN CURRY

INGREDIENTS

Small piece ginger, roughly chopped

5 cloves garlic, roughly chopped

1 onion, sliced

Oil, for frying

1 tsp turmeric

1 tsp chilli powder (to taste)

3-4 chicken thighs and/or legs

5-6 curry leaves

¾ cup (170g, 6oz) tomato puree

3 potatoes, cut into large chunks

¼ cup (60ml, 2fl oz) chicken stock

1-2 star anise

1 cinnamon stick

Fish sauce, to taste

Fresh herbs and chilli slices, to garnish

METHOD

1. Using a pestle and mortar or a food processor, pound/process the ginger, garlic and onions until a rough paste forms.

2. Heat the oil in a deep frying pan over a medium-high heat. Add the turmeric and chilli powder and fry for 1 minute before adding the ginger, garlic and onions. Fry for 5 minutes or until the onions are soft and golden brown but not burnt.

3. Add the chicken and fry, turning frequently, for 5 minutes, until seared. Add curry leaves and stir through.

4. Add the tomato puree and stir to combine. Add the potatoes, chicken stock, star anise and cinnamon. Allow to simmer for 15 minutes. Taste and season with fish sauce if required.

SWEET CHICKEN CURRY PIE

INGREDIENTS

225g (8oz) almonds

½ tsp cinnamon

Butter, for frying

1 onion, peeled
and finely chopped

1 rotisserie chicken,
skin removed and meat
shredded

½ tsp pepper

Pinch of saffron

¾ cup (30g, 1oz)
fresh parsley, chopped

¼ cup (10g, ¼ oz)
fresh coriander, chopped

3 eggs, beaten

¼ cup (195g, 6½ oz)
icing sugar

Salt and pepper, to taste

Prepared shortcrust
pastry dough

Melted butter, for brushing

Icing sugar, to garnish

Whole almonds, to garnish

METHOD

1. Preheat oven to 200°C (400°F, Gas Mark 6) and grease a springform tin.

2. Dry fry almonds in frying pan over medium heat. Grind in a food processor with cinnamon and sugar until a fine breadcrumb consistency. Set aside.

3. Heat butter in a large frying pan over medium-high heat. Add onion and fry until very soft. Add cooked chicken, pepper, saffron, parsley and coriander. Whisk eggs, icing sugar, salt and pepper to taste into the chicken mixture. Bring back to a boil, remove from heat and set aside.

4. Place a sheet of pastry in the bottom of the prepared tin, extending up the sides. Spoon chicken mixture over dough then spread with almond mixture. Add a layer of pastry on top and brush with melted butter.

5. Bake for 35 minutes or until golden. Sprinkle with icing sugar and almonds before serving.

CHICKEN LAKSA

INGREDIENTS

2 tbsps laksa paste

4 cups (1L, 2pt)
chicken stock

1 x 400ml (14fl oz)
can coconut cream

2 chicken breast fillets,
sliced

2 eggs

300g (10oz) noodles

1 tbsp lime juice

1 tbsp fish sauce

1 tsp brown sugar

4 tofu puffs, sliced

Lime wedges,
to garnish

Bean sprouts, to garnish

Red chilli, finely sliced,
to garnish

Curry leaves,
to garnish

METHOD

1. Add laksa paste to a large saucepan and cook over medium heat, stirring, for 1 minute or until fragrant. Stir in chicken stock and coconut cream.

2. Bring to a simmer, add the chicken and cook until just cooked through, approximately 5 minutes.

3. Bring a pan of water to the boil and add eggs. Cook for 7 minutes and then drain and allow eggs to cool before peeling and slicing in half. Set aside.

4. Meanwhile, to cook the noodles place in a large heatproof bowl and cover with boiling water. Stand for 3-4 minutes or until softened. Drain and set aside.

5. Stir the lime juice, fish sauce and brown sugar through the laksa mixture. Add the tofu.

6. To serve, divide noodles between large serving bowls. Pour over the chicken laksa mixture and top with sliced egg, lime wedges, bean sprouts, curry leaves and chilli slices. Serve immediately.

SPICY OKRA AND CHICKEN GUMBO

INGREDIENTS

1 cup (250ml, 8fl oz) vegetable oil

1 cup (125g, 4oz) plain flour

1 onion, diced

3 celery ribs, diced

3 garlic cloves, finely chopped

6 cups (1.5L, 50fl oz) chicken stock

175g (6oz) smoked sausage, sliced

2 bay leaves

2 tbsp prepared jerk paste or 1 tbsp ground jerk seasoning

1 tbsp dried thyme

1 tbsp smoked paprika

400g (14oz) okra, thickly sliced

300g (10oz) cooked shredded chicken

Salt and pepper

METHOD

1. In a large casserole dish, heat oil until very hot. Gradually add the flour, whisking after each addition. When all flour has been incorporated, cook the roux over moderately low heat, whisking often, for 5-10 minutes or until the desired colour and consistency is reached.

2. In a separate pan, fry the onion, celery and garlic and cook over a low-medium heat, stirring occasionally, until the onion is translucent, about 15 minutes. Add to the roux and stir in well.

3. Gradually add the stock to the casserole, whisking until smooth. Add the sausage, bay leaves, jerk paste or seasoning, thyme and paprika and raise the heat to a simmer. Cook over low heat for 45 minutes.

4. Add the okra to the casserole and simmer until tender, 15 minutes. Stir in the chicken meat and season the gumbo with salt and pepper. Discard the bay leaves before serving over rice.

BOMBAY CHICKEN WINGS

INGREDIENTS

12 chicken wings

1 tsp curry powder

½ tsp ground turmeric

1 tsp brown
mustard seeds

1 small red chilli,
finely chopped

2 tbsps soy sauce

2 tbsps vegetable oil

2 tbsps spring onion,
minced

2 cloves garlic,
minced

Pinch of black pepper

METHOD

1. In large bowl, mix together everything apart from the chicken wings to form a marianade.

2. Add chicken wings to the bowl and rub in the marinade, making sure all pieces are coated well. Cover and refrigerate for at least 1 hour.

3. Preheat oven to 175°C (350°F, Gas Mark 4). Drain excess marinade from chicken wings and then place in a single layer baking dish.

4. Transfer to the oven to bake for 25 minutes or until golden brown and cooked through.

BALTI CHICKEN

INGREDIENTS

3 tbsps tomato puree

2 tbsps Greek yoghurt

$1\frac{1}{2}$ tsps garam masala

1 tsp chilli powder

1 tsp minced garlic

2 tbsps mango chutney

1 tsp salt

$\frac{1}{2}$ tsp sugar

4 tbsps oil

4 -6 boneless skinless
chicken breasts, cubed

2 green chillies, chopped

2 tbsps chopped
fresh coriander

2 tbsps cream

Coriander leaves,
to garnish

METHOD

1. Mix together the tomato puree, yoghurt, garam masala, chilli powder, garlic, mango chutney, salt and sugar.

2. Heat the oil in a frying pan and when shimmering add the tomato-spice mixture. Cook for approximately 2 minutes, stirring occasionally.

3. Add the chicken and a dash of cold water, and continue to cook for around 12-15 minutes or until chicken is cooked through, stirring occasionally.

4. Add chillies, fresh coriander and cream, stir in well and cook for a few minutes more.

SERVES 6 ★ PREP 20MIN (PLUS MARINATING) ★ COOK TIME 1HR

CHARRED TANDOORI DRUMSTICKS

INGREDIENTS

1 tbsp paprika

1 tbsp garam masala

1 tbsp ground cumin

1 tbsp ground coriander

½ tsp ground turmeric

½ tsp cayenne pepper

Large piece ginger, roughly chopped

6 garlic cloves, roughly chopped

1 cup (250ml, 8fl oz) thick plain yoghurt

1 lime, juiced and zested

¼ cup (60ml, 2fl oz) vegetable oil

2 tsps salt

12 chicken drumsticks

Chives, to garnish

METHOD

1. Preheat the oven to 230°C (445°F, Gas Mark 8). Line a baking tray with aluminum foil and place a greased oven-proof rack over top.

2. Dry fry the paprika, garam masala, cumin, coriander, turmeric and cayenne pepper over a low heat stirring frequently, for about 2 minutes, until aromatic.

3. Remove from heat and combine spices with the ginger, garlic, yoghurt, lime zest and juice, oil and salt in a blender. Process until smooth.

4. Make 2 or 3 cuts in each drumstick and place in a large bowl. Rub the marinade well into the chicken. Cover and refrigerate for at least 3 hours or overnight.

5. Arrange the chicken on the rack, leaving space between the pieces. Spoon any leftover marinade over the drumsticks. Roast for 45 minutes, turning halfway, until the chicken is golden brown and cooked through.

6. When cooked, char the chicken by placing it under the grill about 6 inches from the heat for 3-5 minutes.

7. Garnish with chives and serve with white rice.

GREEN CHICKEN CURRY

INGREDIENTS

1 x 210ml (7fl oz)
can coconut cream

1½ tbsps green curry paste

8 chicken thigh fillets,
cut into pieces

200g (7oz) pumpkin,
sliced or cubed

6-8 kaffir lime leaves,
torn into strips

1 x 400ml (14fl oz)
can coconut milk

1 bunch bok choy

1 tbsp fish sauce

1 tbsp palm sugar,
finely chopped

½ cup (10g, ¼ oz) fresh
Thai basil leaves

Sliced red chilli, to serve

METHOD

1. Pour the coconut cream into a wok or pan over a medium-high heat. Bring to the boil and then reduce heat. Simmer for 5 minutes or until the cream almost separates. Stir in the curry paste and cook for a further 2 minutes or until aromatic.

2. Add the chicken, pumpkin, kaffir lime leaves and coconut milk and stir. Reduce to a low heat for 10 minutes stirring occasionally, until the chicken is cooked through and the sauce thickens slightly.

3. Add the bok choy and cook, stirring occasionally, for 2 minutes or until the vegetables are tender. Remove from heat.

4. Add the fish sauce, palm sugar and half the basil to the curry mixture and stir.

5. Spoon the curry into bowls and top with the remaining basil and sliced red chilli. Serve on top of steamed jasmine rice, if desired.

EASY TANDOORI CHICKEN

INGREDIENTS

1 lemon, juiced

2 tsp paprika

1 red onion, finely chopped

8 skinless chicken thighs

$^2/_3$ cup (150ml, 5fl oz) plain thick yoghurt

Medium piece ginger, grated

2 garlic cloves, crushed

½ tsp garam masala

½ tsp ground cumin

¼ tsp chilli powder

½ tsp turmeric

Vegetable oil, for brushing

METHOD

1. Combine the lemon juice, paprika and red onions in a large shallow dish. Cut each chicken thigh three times with a sharp knife, then turn them in the juice and set aside for 10 mins.

2. Mix the yoghurt, ginger, garlic, garam masala, cumin, chilli powder and turmeric together and rub over the chicken. Cover and refrigerate for at least 1 hour or up to 24 hours before cooking the chicken.

3. Heat the grill or BBQ. Place the chicken pieces onto a rack over a baking tray. Brush over a little oil and grill for 8 mins on each side or until lightly charred and cooked through.

CHICKEN AND POTATO CURRY

INGREDIENTS

1 tbsp sunflower oil

6 chicken thigh fillets, skin on

1 onion, coarsley chopped

2 tbsps mild curry paste

2 large potatoes, cut into chunks

1 tomato, roughly chopped

2 cups (500ml, 1pt) water

METHOD

1. Heat the oil in a large frying pan until shimmering. Add chicken thighs and cook for 2-3 minutes each side until lightly browned. Remove from pan.

2. Return the frying pan to heat and add onion. Cook over a medium-low heat for 5-7 minutes until soft. Stir in the curry paste and cook for 2-3 minutes until fragrant. Add tomato and water and stir to combine.

3. Add the potatoes to the pan and bring to a boil. Reduce heat and return chicken to the pan, then gently simmer for 20-25 minutes or until the chicken is cooked through. Check frequently and add more water if more liquid is required.

SERVES 6 ★ PREP 20MIN **★ COOK TIME 45**MIN

CHICKEN JALFREZI

INGREDIENTS

2 tbsps vegetable oil

1 onion, finely chopped

2 cloves garlic, minced

8 skinless chicken thigh fillets, halved

3 tsps ground turmeric

1 tsp chilli powder

1 tsp salt

1 x 400g (14oz) can diced tomatoes

2 tbsps butter or ghee

3 tsps ground cumin

3 tsps ground coriander

2 tbsps ginger, grated

1 cup (250ml, 8fl oz) plain yoghurt, to serve

Fresh pepper, to garnish

½ cup (20g; ¾ oz) chopped coriander leaves, to serve

METHOD

1. Heat the oil in a large frying pan over medium-high heat. Add onions and cook for about 2 minutes until they start to soften, then add the garlic and cook for a further minute. Add the chicken, turmeric, chilli powder and salt. Fry gently, turning the chicken frequently and ensuring the onion mix does not stick to the pan.

2. Pour in the tomatoes and then simmer, covered, over a medium heat for 20 minutes. Uncover, and simmer for another 10 minutes and let the liquid evapourate to the desired thickness and consistency.

3. Add the ghee, cumin, coriander, ginger and half the coriander leaves, and simmer for another 5 to 7 minutes.

4. Add a dollop of Greek yoghurt, the remaining coriander leaves and ground pepper to each plate, and serve with pilau rice.

DORO WAT (ETHIOPIAN CURRY)

INGREDIENTS

Spiced butter

450g (1lb) butter

1 tbsp ginger, chopped

1 tsp ground allspice

1 tsp fenugreek seeds

1 tsp dried oregano

½ tsp turmeric

6 cardamom pods, crushed

2 cloves garlic, chopped

1 onion, chopped

Marinade

8 chicken thighs

1 lemon, juiced

1 tsp salt

Curry

Oil, for frying

2 onions, finely diced

¼ cup (25g, 1oz) berbere spice mix

1 tbsp garlic, minced

Small piece ginger, minced

1 tbsp tomato paste

1¼ cups (310ml, 10fl oz) chicken stock

METHOD

1. To make the spiced butter, melt butter in a small saucepan. Stir in ginger, allspice, fenugreek, oregano, turmeric, cardamom, garlic and onions and simmer for 30 minutes until butter is clear and milk solids remain on the bottom of the pan. Remove from heat. Line a strainer with a cheesecloth or use a fine-mesh sieve. Skim the foam from the top of the butter and discard. Ladle the butter through the strainer, leaving behind the milk solids on the bottom of the pan.

2. Marinate chicken in lemon juice and salt. Cover and leave to stand at room temperature for 30 minutes.

3. Heat the oil in a frying pan over a medium-high heat. Add the and fry for 10 minutes, stirring constantly, until golden. Add $1/3$ cup (80ml, 3fl oz) of the spiced butter, the berbere mix, garlic, ginger and tomato paste and cook, stirring, for 1 minute. Add chicken, and stir to coat well with the spice and onion mix.

4. Add chicken stock. Cover, reduce the heat and cook at a gentle simmer for 40 minutes or until chicken is tender. Remove lid and cook for a further 45 minute, until sauce is very thick.

5. Remove from the heat and add the eggs, turning to coat them in the sauce. Cover the pan and let rest for 5 minutes. Serve.

CHICKEN NOODLE KHAO SOI

INGREDIENTS

125g (4½ oz) dried egg noodles

½ cup (125ml, 4fl oz) vegetable oil

Oil, for frying

2 tbsps yellow curry paste

1 cup (250ml, 8fl oz) coconut milk

1½ cups (375ml, 13fl oz) chicken stock or water

2 tbsps palm sugar

2 chicken thighs

1-2 tbsps fish sauce

Coriander leaves, to garnish

METHOD

1. Soak ¼ of the noodles in hot water until they begin to soften and then drain.

2. Heat the vegetable oil in a wok or frying pan and cook the softened noodles until crispy. Remove and put on paper towel to absorb excess oil.

3. Heat some oil in the same pan. Add the curry paste and 2 tablespoon of coconut cream from the top of the coconut milk. Stir-fry until fragrant.

4. Add the rest of the coconut milk, stock and palm sugar. Stir to combine and then add the chicken pieces. Bring the curry soup to a boil, then turn heat down to simmer for 30-40 minutes or until the meat is soft and tender.

5. In the meantime, cook the remaining noodles in boiling water according to the instructions on the packet. When cooked, divide the noodles into serving bowls.

6. Once the chicken is tender, stir the fish sauce into the soup. Add more palm sugar for sweetness or more fish sauce for saltiness.

7. Place the chicken with the cooked egg noodles and pour over the coconut curry soup.

8. Top each bowl with crispy noodles and garnish with coriander.

MEAT

Lamb rogan josh   58

Pork tonkatsu   60

Simple beef samosa   62

Kofta in tomato sauce   63

Slow beef madras   64

Curried meatball sandwich   66

Beef massaman curry   68

Bunny chow   70

Beef curry benedict   71

Coconut beef curry   72

Jamaican jerk patty   74

Meatballs in curry sauce   76

Mutton and tomato curry   78

Kerala fried beef   79

Beef rendang   80

South African bobotie   82

Thai-style pork curry   84

Pad kee mao drunken noodle   86

Easy crockpot lamb and pumpkin curry   87

Spiced beef stew with pomegranate   88

Moroccan meatballs   90

Lamb and apple curry pita   92

Simple pork curry   93

Spiced lamb chops   94

Pork Penang   96

Jamaican pumpkin and pork curry   98

Curry wurst with french fries   100

Pork, eggplant and red lentil curry   101

Japanese curry rice with cheese and fried egg   102

Vietnamese beef pho   104

Spicy mapo tofu   106

LAMB ROGAN JOSH

INGREDIENTS

Medium piece fresh ginger, coarsely chopped

8 garlic cloves, peeled

4 tbsps water

¼ cup (60ml, 2fl oz) vegetable oil or ghee

1kg (2lb) boneless lamb shoulder, cubed

10 cardamom pods

2 bay leaves

6 whole cloves

8-10 peppercorns

1 cinnamon stick

4 medium onions, finely chopped

1 tsp ground coriander

2 tsps cumin seeds (or ground cumin)

4 tsps ground paprika

1 tsp cayenne pepper

1 tsp salt

6 tbsps plain yoghurt

1¼ cups (275ml, 9fl oz) water

METHOD

1. Put the ginger, garlic and water into the blender. Blend to a smooth paste.

2. Heat oil or ghee in a heavy pot over a medium-high heat. Brown the meat in serveral batches and set aside.

3. Using the same pan, add the cardamom, bay leaves, cloves, peppercorns and cinnamon into the hot oil. Stir once and leave to cook for 1 minutes, then add the onions. Fry, stirring, for 5 minutes until onions are soft and golden. Add the ginger and garlic and stir for 30 seconds Then add the coriander, cumin, paprika, cayenne and salt. Stir-fry for 30 seconds. Add the meat and stir for 30 seconds.

4   Add 1 tablespoon of the yoghurt, and stir until well combined. Add the remaining yoghurt a tablespoon at a time in the same way. Cook, stirring occassionally, for another 3 minutes.

5. Add the water. Bring to the boil, scraping all the browned spices off the sides and bottom of the pot. Cover and cook on a low heat, stirring occasionally, for an hour or until lamb is tender. Add more water during cooking if mixture looks to be drying out. When the meat is tender, turn the heat up to medium, and boil away any excess liquid. Remove cinammon stick before serving.

PORK TONKATSU

INGREDIENTS

Sauce

¼ cup (60ml, 2fl oz) tomato ketchup

3 tbsps Worcestershire sauce

2 tbsps oyster sauce

4 tsps sugar

1 tsp salt

1 tsp Dijon mustard

Pork

4 boneless pork loin chops

½ cup (60g, 2oz) plain flour

1 egg, beaten

1½ cups (185g, 6oz) panko breadcrumbs

Oil, for frying

Seaweed, to garnish

4 poached eggs

METHOD

1. Combine sauce ingredients in a small bowl and whisk together. Set aside.

2. Between two sheets of plastic wrap, pound the chops with a rolling pin to about 5mm (¼ in) thick. Sprinkle with salt and pepper.

3. Toss pork chops in flour, dip in the beaten egg, then immediately coat both sides in panko breadcrumbs. Press breadcrumbs onto the meat, then set aside for a few minutes.

4. Heat the oil in a frying pan over medium-high heat. When shimmering, carefully add the pork chops. Fry in batches for 3 minutes each side or until deep golden brown, then turn and fry the other side. Drain on paper towels.

5. To serve, cover the bottom of a plate or bowl with the sauce, lay over the pork and sprinkle with seaweed. Serve with a poached egg.

SIMPLE BEEF SAMOSA

INGREDIENTS

1 tbsp olive oil

500g (1lb) beef mince

1 onion, finely chopped

2 cloves garlic, crushed

1 tsp ground cumin

1 tsp ground coriander

1 tsp ground turmeric

1 tsp grated ginger

2 potatoes, finely diced

20 spring roll wrappers

Oil, for frying

Lemon wedges and mint, to garnish

METHOD

1. Heat oil on a high temperature in a large frying pan. Add the mince and fry until browned. Reduce heat and stir in onion, garlic, cumin, coriander, turmeric, ginger and potato. Cook, stirring from time to time for 5 minutes, or until potatoes are just tender. Allow mixture to cool.

2. Place a mound of filling in one corner of a spring roll wrapper, leaving a thumb's width around the edge.

3. Fold the pastry corner diagonally to create a triangle, then continue to wrap, in the triangle shape. Continue until you have run out of fillling and/or wrappers.

4. Heat oil to a depth of 2cm (1in) in a deep-sided frying pan or saucepan. Quickly cook samosa in batches until crisp and golden on both sides. Transfer to a paper-towel-lined plate, and allow oil to absorb before serving.

KOFTA IN TOMATO SAUCE

INGREDIENTS

Kofta

450g (1lb) beef mince

2 onions, chopped

Small piece ginger, minced

1 garlic clove, minced

1 tsp cumin seeds

1 tsp garam masala

1 tsp ground coriander

1 green chilli, chopped

Curry

Oil for frying

1 tsp cumin seeds

3 cloves

1 cinnamon stick

3 green cardamom pods

2 onions, chopped

Small piece ginger

2 garlic cloves, minced

4 tomatoes, chopped

1 tsp garam masala

½ tsp chilli powder

1 tbsp ground coriander

¼ tsp ground turmeric

1 cup (250ml, 8fl oz) water

Coriander and yoghurt
to garnish

METHOD

1. Combine the kofta ingredients in a large bowl. Roll into meatballs. Set aside.

2. Heat oil in a frying pan and add the meatballs, frying until golden brown. Remove from the oil and leave to drain on paper towel.

3. Heat oil in a saucepan. Add cumin seeds, cloves, cinnamon stick and cardamom pods. When cumin seeds start to sizzle add chopped onions and fry for 5 minutes or until onion starts to brown. Add ginger and garlic and fry for 1 minute.

4. Stir in tomatoes and powdered spices. Cook until soft and mixture starts to separate from oil.

5. Add water and bring curry to the boil. Lower the heat and bring to a gentle simmer for 10 minutes. Garnish with fresh coriander leaves and a spoonful of yoghurt to serve.

SLOW BEEF MADRAS

INGREDIENTS

2 tbsps ground coriander

1 tbsp ground cumin

1 tsp turmeric

½ tsp pepper

1 tsp chilli powder

3 garlic cloves, crushed

1 tbsp ginger, grated

2½ tbsps lemon juice

2 tbsps olive oil

1kg (2lb) chuck steak, cubed

2 tomatoes, chopped

2 tbsps tomato paste

1 cup (250ml, 8fl oz) beef stock

Steamed basmati rice, to serve

Coriander leaves, to serve

METHOD

1. Combine coriander, cumin, turmeric, pepper, chilli, garlic, ginger and lemon juice in a bowl to form a paste (or use a food processor to complete this step). Set aside.

2. Heat 1 tablespoon oil in a large saucepan over high heat. Add half the steak. Cook, stirring frequently, until the meat has browned. This should take 2-3 minutes. Transfer to a bowl. Repeat with second batch of oil and beef.

3. Reduce heat to medium. Add spice paste and cook for 1 minute. Return beef to saucepan and cook, stirring, for 1 minute, or until meat is coated with paste. Add the tomatoes, tomato paste and stock and bring to the boil. Reduce heat to low. Cover and cook for 1 hour 45 minutes, or until beef is tender.

4. Remove the lid from the pan and cook, uncovered, for a further 15 minutes, or until sauce has reduced and thickened to the desired consistency.

5. Serve with steamed basmati rice and garnish with coriander.

CURRIED MEATBALL SANDWICH

INGREDIENTS

Meatballs

500g (1lb) beef mince

1 onion, chopped

¼ tsp salt

¼ tsp black pepper

2 tbsps fresh breadcrumbs

2 tbsps plain flour

Oil, for frying

Curry Sauce

1 onion, chopped

1 tbsp curry powder

1 tbsp tomato paste

2 tbsps lemon juice

1¼ cups (325ml, 11fl oz) water

Salt and pepper, to taste

4 toasted naans

METHOD

1. In a large bowl combine mince with onion, salt, pepper, breadcrumbs and flour. Shape into 12-16 balls and roll in flour.

2. Heat oil in a frying pan over a medium-high heat. Add meatballs and fry, turning with tongs, to ensure even browning. Set aside.

3. Using fresh oil in the same pan, saute onion for 5 minutes or until translucent, then add curry powder.

4. Stir in tomato paste, lemon juice and water. Season with salt and pepper and bring to the boil.

5. Add meatballs to sauce and gently simmer for 20 minutes.

6. Serve meatballs in toasted naan breads covered with curry sauce.

BEEF MASSAMAN CURRY

INGREDIENTS

Paste

1 red onion, chopped

2 red chillies, chopped

2 tsps ground coriander

2 tsps cumin

3 cloves garlic, peeled

1 lemongrass, pale part only, trimmed and chopped

Medium piece ginger, chopped

1 tsp shrimp paste

3 tsps fish sauce

1 tsp brown sugar

10 fresh coriander stalks

Curry

1kg (2lb) beef, sliced

1 onion, chopped

1½ tbsps cornflour

2 tbsps vegetable oil

1²/₃ cups (390ml, 13fl oz) beef or chicken stock

1 x 400ml (14fl oz) can coconut milk

2 potatoes, quartered

2 carrots, sliced

METHOD

1. Place paste ingredients in a food processor and process until a smooth paste forms. Set aside.

2. Toss beef in the cornflour and season with salt and pepper. Heat the oil in a large, heavy-based pan on a medium-high heat. Fry the meat in the oil for about 5 minutes until brown, stirring to ensure it doesn't stick. Set aside.

3. Heat oil over a medium high heat using the same pan. Add onion and fry for 5 minutes until soft.

4. Reduce heat to medium-low and stir in the curry paste, cooking for 2-3 minutes. Add in the stock and coconut milk. Stir and cover. Gently simmer on a low heat for 1 hour and 25 minutes. Check consistency occasionally during cooking and add more liquid if required. If you want to reduce the liquid, remove the lid and continue cooking.

5. Add potatoes and carrots and cook for a further 25 minutes until tender.

6. Serve with basmati rice and garnish with a handful of peanuts and coriander leaves.

BUNNY CHOW

INGREDIENTS

Oil, for frying

1kg (2lb) boneless leg of lamb, cubed

1 onion, chopped

3 garlic cloves, crushed

Medium piece ginger, grated

1 star anise

1 cinnamon stick

½ tsp fennel seeds

2 tsps garam masala

¼ tsp chilli powder

1 tbsp tomato paste

2 cups (500ml, 1pt) chicken stock

1 x 400g (14oz) can butter beans, drained

$^1/_3$ cup (80ml, 3fl oz) thick plain yoghurt

4 round bread rolls

Olive oil, to brush

METHOD

1. Preheat the oven to 180°C (350°F, Gas Mark 4).

2. Heat oil in large saucepan over medium heat. Add chicken and cook, turning, for 4-5 minutes until browned. Set chicken aside.

3. Add onion and cook, stirring, for 3-4 minutes until softened. Add garlic, ginger and spices, and cook for 2 minutes or until fragrant. Add tomato paste and cook for 1 minute. Return chicken to pan and add stock. Bring to a simmer, then reduce heat to medium-low and cook for 20 minutes.

4. Add beans and cook for 5 minutes or until sauce is thickened. Add yoghurt and stir. Remove from heat.

5. Meanwhile, cut the tops off the rolls and hollow out, discarding filling. Brush with olive oil and bake for 5 minutes or until slightly golden.

6. Place curry inside bread bowls and garnish to serve.

BEEF CURRY BENEDICT

INGREDIENTS

3 tbsps vegetable oil

2 onions, coarsely chopped

1/2 tsp ground cloves

1 tsp ground cinnamon

1/2 tsp ground cardamom

1 tsp ginger, minced

1 tsp garlic, minced

500g (1lb) beef, diced

2 tsps chilli powder

2 tomatoes, pureed

1 potato, peeled and finely diced

Salt, to taste

4 large eggs (poached)

Salad leaves, to garnish

METHOD

1. Heat oil in a saucepan and add the onion. Cook for 5 minutes, stirring, until onion is soft. Add the cloves, cinnamon, cardamom, garlic and ginger and cook for another 2-3 minutes until aromatic.

2. Add the beef and chilli powder and stir well. Cook, stirring occassionally, for a further 3-4 minutes until beef has browned.

3. Add the tomatoes and potatoes, and mix well. Season to taste.

4. Add water to just cover the meat and cook, covered, until for 20 minutes, or until the meat is tender and the gravy is thick. Remove the lid to reduce the gravy, if necessary.

5. Assemble egg on toast with curry and salad to garnish.

SERVES 4 ★ PREP 20MIN ★ COOK TIME 1HR 10MIN

COCONUT BEEF CURRY

INGREDIENTS

1 star anise

2 cloves

10 curry leaves

3 long green chillies,
roughly chopped

½ tsp turmeric

2 shallots, quartered

4 garlic cloves,
roughly chopped

Small piece ginger,
roughly chopped

1 tsp salt

1 tbsp vegetable oil

Coconut oil, for frying

500g (1lb) chuck steak,
cubed

1 cup (250ml, 8fl oz)
coconut water (or stock)

1 cinnamon stick

½ cup (40g, 1½ oz)
freshly gated coconut
(or desiccated coconut)

1 x 400ml (14fl oz)
tin coconut milk

METHOD

1. Preheat the oven to 150°C (300°F, Gas Mark 2).

2. Place star anise, cloves and curry leaves in a food processor
    and pulse until roughly ground. Add chillies, turmeric, shallots,
    garlic, ginger and salt and process until a thick paste starts
    to form. Then add the oil and continue to process into a
    curry paste.

3. Heat coconut oil in a large, heavy-based saucepan on a
    medium-high heat. Add the beef and brown in batches if
    necessary, removing from the pan after each batch is browned.
    Set beef aside.

4. Heat coconut oil in the same pan and add the curry paste.
    Fry for 1-2 minutes until aromatic.

5. Add the coconut water or stock and stir to deglaze the pan.

6. Place the meat and juices back in the pot. Add cinnamon stick,
    fresh or desicated coconut and coconut milk.

7. Bring to a boil, then cover and place in the oven to cook for
    1 hour or until the meat is tender.

8. Remove from the oven. Season to taste and garnish with
    slices of red chilli and coriander to serve.

JAMAICAN JERK PATTY

INGREDIENTS

2 cups (250g, 8oz)
plain flour

½ tbsp curry powder

¼ tsp salt

¼ cup (4 tbsps) solid
shortening

¼ cup (4 tbsps) cold butter

⅓ cup (80ml, 3fl oz)
icy cold water

2 tbsps butter

1 small onion, chopped

¼ tsp chopped Scotch
bonnet chilli

250g (9oz) beef mince

½ tsp curry powder

½ tsp dried thyme,
crushed

½ tsp ground allspice

½ tsp salt

½ tsp ground black pepper

¼ cup (30g, 1oz)
breadcrumbs

¼ cup (60ml, 2fl oz)
beef stock

¼ cup (60ml, 2fl oz) water

1 egg, beaten

METHOD

1. Preheat oven to 200°C (400°F, Gas Mark 6). Line two baking trays with greaseproof paper.

2. Combine flour, curry powder, and salt in the bowl of a food processor fitted with a metal blade. Add shortening and butter. Pulse until mixture is crumbly. Add cold water and pulse until a dough just forms.

2. Roll dough on a floured surface. Cut into circles and place on a floured tray or board. Cover with plastic wrap until ready to use.

3. Meanwhile, heat butter in frying pan over medium heat and fry onion and chilli until softened. Add beef, curry powder, thyme, allspice, salt and pepper and cook for 10 minutes, stirring often.

4. Add breadcrumbs and beef stock to the pan. Cover and simmer 10 minutes, stirring occasionally, until all the liquid has been absorbed but the mixture has not completely dried out. Remove from heat and cool for 10 minutes.

5. Place 3 tablespoons of the meat filling in the center of each pastry circle. Moisten the edges of the circles, fold in half, and press to seal. Mix remaining water with the egg. Brush the tops of the patties with the egg wash.

6. Bake for 30 minutes until golden.

MEATBALLS IN CURRY SAUCE

INGREDIENTS

Meatballs

700g (1½lb) ground beef

1 onion, finely chopped

1 small red chilli (optional)

2 tbsps garam masala

2 tbsps curry powder

Small piece fresh
ginger, grated

1 egg

Curry Sauce

1 tbsp oil

1 onion, finely chopped

2 cloves garlic, minced

3 tbsps curry powder

2 tbsps garam masala

1 tbsp ginger, grated

1 tsp turmeric

1 tsp ground coriander

1½ cups (375ml, 13fl oz)
coconut milk

1 cup (250ml, 8fl oz)
chicken stock

Parsley, to garnish

Red chilli, to garnish

METHOD

1. Preheat oven to 200°C (400°F, Gas Mark 6).

2. Place the ingredients for the meatballs together in a large bowl and combine thoroughly. Roll into walnut-sized balls, and place the meatballs on a lined baking tray.

3. Transfer to the oven and bake for 15-20 minutes, until cooked through.

4. Meanwhile, heat the oil in a large frying pan over medium-high heat. When hot, add the onions and fry until soft, approximately 5-7 minutes. Next add the garlic and fry for 1 minute until fragrant. Then add curry powder, garam masala, ginger, turmeric and coriander and fry the spices for 1 minute.

5. Add the coconut milk and chicken stock into the frying pan and whisk to combine. Bring the sauce to a boil, and cook for 5-10 minutes.

6. Add the cooked meatballs to the sauce, stirring to coat. Serve with rice and garnish with parsley and slices of red chilli.

MUTTON AND TOMATO CURRY

INGREDIENTS

3 tbsps oil

2 onions, chopped

5 green chillies, slit

3 tbsps garlic-ginger paste

1 tsp chilli powder

1 tsp allspice powder

2 tbsps ground coriander

1 tsp ground turmeric

1kg (2lb) mutton, cubed and washed

Salt, to taste

2 tbsps coriander leaves, chopped

6 small tomatoes, halved

Fresh coriander, to garnish

METHOD

1. In a heavy-based saucepan, heat the oil on a medium heat. Add onions and fry for 10 minutes or until golden brown. Add the chillies and ginger-garlic paste and saute for a further 3 minutes.

2. Add the chilli powder, allspice, ground coriander and turmeric and fry for a further 3 minutes. Continue to fry the mixture till the oil begins to leave the paste.

3. Add mutton and fry until browned and coated in spice mix. Add salt to taste and water to cover the meat. Stir in the coriander leaves and reduce heat to a low simmer. Cover and cook for 1 hour, 20 minutes or until the mutton is tender.

4. Stir in tomatoes about 5 minutes before curry is ready. Serve garnished with coriander.

KERALA FRIED BEEF

INGREDIENTS

1kg (2lb) beef chuck steak, cubed

2 cups (500ml, 1pt) water

1 tsp salt

¼ tsp ground turmeric

Medium piece ginger, coarsely chopped

5 green chillies, slit

3 tbsps vegetable oil

¼ cup (20g, ¾ oz) coconut flakes

2 onions, roughly chopped

1 tbsp ground coriander

1 tsp chilli powder

1 tsp ground turmeric

2 stems curry leaves, leaves picked

1 tomato, chopped

1 tsp garam masala

1 tsp ground black pepper

METHOD

1. Cook the beef for 15-20 minutes (or until about half the liquid remains) in a pressure cooker with water, salt, ground turmeric, ginger and green chilli.

2. Heat the oil in a large, non-stick, shallow-rimmed frying pan. Fry the coconut flakes and onion together until light brown.

3. Stir in the ground coriander, chilli powder and ground turmeric and saute on a low heat.

4. Add the curry leaves followed by the chopped tomato and saute until the oil clears.

5. Add in the garam masala, pepper and cooked beef with water, and stir occasionally until the gravy evapourates.

6. Keep on a low heat and cook for a few more minutes until the beef is browned.

BEEF RENDANG

INGREDIENTS

120g (4oz)
desiccated coconut

1 tsp salt

2 tsps sugar

2 tsps tamarind paste

500g (1lb) beef chuck
steak, cubed

2 onions

3 jalapeño chillies

6-8 dried chillies

1 medium piece ginger

1 stalk lemongrass, crushed

1 small piece galangal
(or ginger), sliced

3 cloves garlic

1 tbsp oil

1 tsp ground turmeric

2-3 kaffir lime leaves, sliced

2 tbsps palm sugar

1 tsp salt

½ tsp white pepper

3 tsps dark soy sauce

1 x 400ml (14fl oz) can
coconut cream

METHOD

1. In a large frying pan over a medium-high heat, dry fry the
    coconut until golden brown.

2. In a large bowl mix the salt, sugar and tamarind paste together
    and toss the beef cubes in this mixture. Then add the toasted
    coconut. Set aside.

3. Place onions, chillies, ginger, lemongrass and garlic in a food
    processor and pulse until a fine paste forms. Set aside.

4. Heat the oil in a large saucepan over medium heat. Then add
    the spice paste mixture and cook for 1-2 minutes until aromatic.
    Add turmeric, kaffir lime leaves, galangal (or ginger), palm sugar,
    salt, pepper and soy sauce and cook, stirring, for 3 minutes.

5. Add the beef and stir for a further 2 minutes, then add the
    coconut cream. Reduce to a gentle simmer, cover and cook for
    1 hour or until meat is tender.

SOUTH AFRICAN BOBOTIE

INGREDIENTS

2 slices white bread

1½ cups (375ml, 13fl oz) milk, divided

Oil, for frying

1 onion, chopped

3 tsps curry powder

1 tbsp breyani masala (or garam masala)

1 tsp turmeric

1 tomato, chopped

½ tsp sugar

1 apple, peeled and coarsely grated

1 tbsp orange rind, grated

¼ cup (40g, 1½ oz) seedless raisins (optional)

750g (1½lb) minced beef or lamb

2 tsps salt

2 tbsps apricot jam

1 egg

Handful of almonds

Tumeric custard

1 egg

½ cup (125ml, 4fl oz) milk

½ tsp tumeric

METHOD

1. Preheat oven to 180°C (350°F, Gas Mark 4) and grease a glass oven dish.

2. In a small bowl, tear up the slices of bread roughly. Pour half the milk over the bread. Set aside.

3. Heat oil in a large pot. Add onion and fry over medium heat until translucent. Add the curry powder, breyani masala and turmeric. Stir, and let the spices cook for 2-3 minutes. Add tomato, sugar, grated apple, lemon rind and raisins, if using, and stir to combine. Fry for a minute, then add the meat, breaking to loosen. Add salt. Cook for 5 minutes, stirring constantly, until mince is browned. Add the apricot jam, and stir so it melts into the meat mixture. Cook for a further 5 minutes.

4. Remove from heat and allow to cool slightly. Break the bread up into wet crumbs. Add the milky crumbs to the meat mixture, and mix through.

5. Break egg into a small bowl. Add the other half of the milk and whisk to combine. Add milk-egg mixture to the meat.

6. Spoon mixture into oven dish, and stud with almonds. Transfer to oven to cook for 40 minutes.

7. Whisk the other egg with the milk and turmeric to make a custard mix.

8. Remove meat from the oven and pour over the custard. Return to oven to cook for a further 15 minutes, or until the egg custard has set.

THAI-STYLE PORK CURRY

INGREDIENTS

2 tbsps cumin seeds

1½ tbsps coriander seeds

1½ tbsps fenugreek seeds

1 tbsp black peppercorns

3 tsps whole cloves

4 cinnamon sticks

1½ tbsps ground turmeric

½ tsp ground nutmeg

6 Thai red chillies (to taste)

6 lemongrass stalks, pale part, thinly sliced

3 Asian shallots, chopped

6 garlic cloves, chopped

Small piece galangal (or ginger), chopped

2 tsps dried shrimp paste

1 tsp salt

1kg (2lb) boneless pork belly, rind removed, cubed

1 tsp salt

10 Asian shallots, peeled

Medium piece ginger, sliced

2 tbsps tamarind concentrate

2 tbsps grated palm sugar

METHOD

1. Place cumin, coriander and fenugreek seeds, peppercorns, cloves and cinnamon in a frying pan over a low heat. Toast, stirring, for 3 minutes or until fragrant. Stir in turmeric and nutmeg. Remove from the heat and set the spice mix aside. Remove cinnamon sticks.

2. Blend chillies, lemongrass, shallots, garlic, galangal or ginger, shrimp paste and salt in a food processor. Add a little water if required to make a curry paste.

3. Place pork in a bowl with curry paste and rub paste into pork. Add salt and spice mix, and rub to coat the pork.

4. Place a heavy-based saucepan over high heat. Add pork and cook, turning occasionally, for 8 minutes or until lightly browned. Add 4 cups (1L, 2pt) water, or enough to cover, and bring to the boil. Stir in shallots and ginger. Reduce heat to low and cook for 2 hours or until pork is very tender.

5. Season to taste with 1 tablespoon salt, tamarind and sugar.

PAD KEE MAO DRUNKEN NOODLE

INGREDIENTS

450g (1lb) wide rice noodles

4 tbsps fish sauce

2 tbsps dark sweet soy sauce

1 tsp rice vinegar

6 cloves garlic

5 Thai chillies

3 tbsps vegetable oil

1 onion, sliced

500g (1lb) beef, sliced

1 green capsicum, sliced

1 red capsicum, sliced

1 head broccoli, cut into florets

200g (7oz) snow peas

Lime wedges and basil leaves, to garnish

METHOD

1. Soak the rice noodles in warm water for 30 minutes.

2. Stir together the fish sauce, soy sauce and vinegar, and set aside. Roughly chop the garlic and 3 of the chillies together. Chop the other two chillies, and set aside.

3. Heat a wok or large frying pan over medium-high heat; when hot, add the oil, the garlic/chilli mixture and the onion. Cook, stirring constantly, for about 30 seconds.

4. Add the beef and a splash of the sauce. Stir-fry until cooked through, about 5 minutes.

5. Drain the noodles and add them with the capsicum to the pan. Increase the heat to high, and add the sauce, broccoli and snow peas. Cook until all ingredients are coated with the sauce and vegetables are just tender. Serve with reserved chilli, if desired.

SERVES 4 ★ PREP 15MIN ★ COOK TIME 6-8HR

EASY CROCKPOT LAMB AND PUMPKIN CURRY

INGREDIENTS

1kg (2lb) lean lamb, cubed

3 tbsps curry powder

1 tsp dried oregano

2 hot chillies, chopped (optional)

1 onion, minced

1 carrot, chopped

4 cloves garlic, minced

500g (1lb) pumpkin, cubed

1 x 400g (14oz) can chopped tomatoes

2 bay leaves

4 tbsps crunchy peanut butter

1 tbsp lemon juice

1 x 400ml (14fl oz) can coconut milk

Coriander leaves, to garnish

METHOD

1. Combine all ingredients in the crock pot except the peanut butter, lemon juice and coconut milk.

2. Cook on high for 6 hours or on low for 8.

3. During the last 30 minutes of cooking stir in the peanut butter, lemon juice and coconut milk.

4. Cook for another 30 minutes.

SPICED BEEF STEW WITH POMEGRANATE

INGREDIENTS

2 cups (250g, 8oz) walnut halves

2 tbsps unsalted butter

3 tbsps olive oil

1kg (2lb) beef, cubed

Salt

2 onions, chopped

2 cups (500ml, 1pt) beef stock

1 tbsp candied orange peel, finely chopped

1 tbsp sugar

½ tsp turmeric

¼ tsp cinnamon

¼ tsp ground nutmeg

¼ tsp ground black pepper

5 tbsps pomegranate molasses

Fresh pomegranate seeds, to garnish

METHOD

1. Preheat the oven to 180°C (350°F, Gas Mark 4). Spread the walnuts in a single layer on a baking tray, and place in the oven to toast for 8 to 10 minutes. When cool, grind walnuts in a food processor or blender to a fine consistency.

2. In a large pan, heat 1 tablespoon of the butter and 2 tablespoons of the olive oil over medium-high heat. Brown the beef pieces on all sides, sprinkling with salt during the cooking. If necessary, batch the cooking of the beef so that the pan is not overcrowded. Remove the beef and set aside.

3. Add the remaining butter and oil to the pan. Lower the heat to medium-low. Add chopped onions to the pan and fry until translucent. Return the beef to the pan. Add the stock and bring to a boil. Then reduce heat, cover the pot, and simmer gently for 30 minutes.

4. Stir in orange peel, ground walnuts, sugar, spices and pomegranate molasses. Cover and cook on very low heat for 1 hour, stirring occasionally.

5. Remove from heat and adjust sugar and salt to taste. The beef should be very tender.

6. Garnish with pomegranate seeds and serve with rice.

MOROCCAN MEATBALLS

INGREDIENTS

500g (1lb) lamb mince

¼ tsp ground cinnamon

¼ tsp ground cumin

¼ tsp cayenne pepper

1 small onion, minced

2 garlic cloves, minced

¼ tsp ground ginger

1 lemon, zested and juiced

1 tsp salt

3 tbsps flat leaf parsley, chopped

Pinch of black pepper

2 tbsps butter or oil

1 onion, sliced

2 dried chilli arbols, chopped (or 1 tsp chilli flakes)

Small piece ginger, minced

¼ tsp ground turmeric

¼ cup (10g, ¼ oz) coriander leaves, chopped

1¼ cups (310ml, 10fl oz) water

METHOD

1. In a large bowl, mix together lamb mince, cinnamon, cumin, cayenne pepper, minced onion, minced garlic, ground ginger, lemon zest, salt, parsley and black pepper. Roll the mixture into meatballs to the desired size.

2. Melt the butter or oil in a large pan over medium heat. Add onions, dried chillies or chilli flakes, ginger and ground turmeric. Cook, stirring occasionally, for 5 minutes or until onions are golden brown.

3. Add the coriander, lemon juice and water and stir to combine. Bring the sauce to a boil. Reduce the heat to medium-low, add meatballs, and cover the pot. Cook for 20 minutes.

4. Remove lid and continue cooking for another 10 minutes so that sauce thickens and meatballs are cooked through. Taste and season as needed.

5. Serve with couscous.

LAMB AND APPLE CURRY PITA

INGREDIENTS

Olive oil, for frying

1kg (2lb) lamb shoulder, cubed

2 onions, finely chopped

3 garlic cloves, minced

2 tsp ginger, freshly grated

1 tbsp ground cumin

1 tbsp ground coriander

1 tsp ground turmeric

2 cinnamon sticks

1 green chilli, seeded, finely chopped

1 cup (250ml, 8fl oz) thick plain yoghurt

1 apple, chopped

2 cups (500ml, 1pt) water

Salt and pepper, to taste

Pita bread, to serve

Fresh coriander, to garnish

METHOD

1. Preheat oven to 150°C (300°F, Gas Mark 2).

2. Heat oil in a flameproof casserole dish over a high heat. Add lamb and cook until browned. Remove from pan and set aside.

3. Reduce heat to medium and heat fresh oil in the same pan. Add onion and cook for 5 minutes, stirring occasionally, until translucent. Add garlic and ginger and cook for 1 minute until fragrant, then add cumin, coriander, turmeric, cinnamon and chilli. Cook for 2 minutes, stirring constantly.

4. Return the lamb to the pan with the yoghurt, apple and water and stir to combine. Remove from the heat, cover with lid and place in oven for 2 hours.

5. Season to taste with salt and pepper. Serve inside pita bread garnished with sprig of coriander.

SIMPLE PORK CURRY

INGREDIENTS

1 tsp ground cumin

1 tsp ground coriander

½ tsp ground cinnamon

¼ tsp ground chilli powder

800g (1¾lb) pork, diced

1 tbsp vegetable oil

1 onion, chopped

1 red capsicum, sliced

2 cloves garlic, chopped

Medium piece ginger, grated

1 tbsp water

1 x 400ml (14fl oz) can coconut milk

2 tbsps brown sugar

1 tsp salt

1 tbsp lemon juice

Salt and pepper, to taste

Coriander leaves, to garnish

METHOD

1. Mix the spices together in a medium bowl. Add the pork and toss to coat with spices.

2. Heat the oil in a large frying pan and cook the pork until browned all over. You may need to do this in two batches, depending on the size of your pan. Remove meat from the pan.

3. In the same pan, add onion, capsicum, garlic, ginger and water. Cook over medium heat until softened, stirring frequently.

4. Return the pork to the pan and then stir in the coconut milk, sugar and salt. Simmer, covered, stirring occasionally, for about 1 hour to 1 hour 30 minutes, or until the pork is very tender and the sauce is thickened.

5. Stir in lemon juice and season to taste with salt and pepper. Garnish with coriander and serve.

SPICED LAMB CHOPS

INGREDIENTS

1 tbsp olive oil

1 tsp ground cumin

1 tsp ground coriander

1 garlic clove, crushed

12 lamb cutlets

1 cup (250ml, 8fl oz) thick plain yoghurt

1 bunch coriander leaves, chopped

Squeeze of fresh lemon

Salt and pepper, to season

Ground cumin, to garnish

METHOD

1. In a mixing bowl, combine the olive oil, ground cumin, ground coriander and garlic. Rub the spice mix well into the cutlets and them place in a dish. Cover and place in the fridge to marinate for 30 minutes or longer if possible.

2. To make the raita, combine the yoghurt, fresh coriander and lemon together. Season with salt and pepper. Refrigerate.

3. Heat a barbecue or chargrill pan on medium-high. Cook the cutlets for 2-3 minutes each side for medium-rare.

4. Rest chops for 2-3 minutes, then sprinkle with ground cumin to serve .

PORK PENANG

INGREDIENTS

4 tbsps oil

3 tbsps red curry paste

400g (14oz) pork,
cut into strips

1 x 400ml (14fl oz)
can coconut milk

4 tbsps fish sauce

2 tsps sugar

1¼ cups (300ml, 10fl oz)
water

4 kaffir lime leaves,
whole

1 kaffir lime leaf,
finely sliced

2 red chillies, thickly sliced

METHOD

1. Heat the oil in a frying pan over a meduim heat. Add the curry paste and fry for 2-3 minutes to release the curry fragrance.

2. Add the pork and fry for a further 2 minutes.

3. Add the coconut milk, fish sauce, sugar and water and stir to combine. Partially cover the pan and cook for 15-20 minutes or until pork is cooked but tender.

4. Serve the curry in a bowl topped with the whole and shredded kaffir lime leaves and chillies.

JAMAICAN PUMPKIN AND PORK CURRY

INGREDIENTS

4 cloves

1 star anise

1 tsp black peppercorns

3 tsps cumin seeds

3 tsps coriander seeds

10 cardamom pods, seeds extracted

50g fresh ginger, roughly chopped

4 garlic cloves, roughly chopped

1 onion, roughly chopped

1 tbsp curry powder

½ tsp salt

2 tbsps oil

800g (1¾lb) lean pork shoulder, cubed

1 large onion, thinly sliced

800g (1¾lb) pumpkin, cubed

1 x 200ml (7fl oz) can coconut milk

1 lime, juiced

Coriander leaves, roughly chopped, to garnish

METHOD

1. Combine the cloves, star anise, peppercorns and the cumin, coriander and cardamom seeds together in a blender and grind to a fine texture. Remove the curry powder and set aside.

2. Place the ginger, garlic and onion in the blender with the curry powder and salt, adding just enough water to form a purée.

3. Heat the oil in a large, wide saucepan. Season the pork with salt and pepper, add to the pan and cook until browned. Turn down the heat and add the curry paste. Cook for 2 minutes, stirring frequently.

4. Add the onion to the pan and cook for 3-5 minutes until softened, then add the pumpkin and cook for a further 5 minutes. Pour in water to just cover the pork and pumpkin. Put the lid on the pan and simmer over a low heat for 20–30 minutes until the pork is tender.

5. Stir in the coconut milk and heat through. Finish with a the lime juice and garnish with coriander.

SERVES 2 ★ PREP 10MIN ★ COOK TIME 20MIN

CURRY WURST WITH FRENCH FRIES

INGREDIENTS

300g (10oz) potatoes

1 tbsp curry powder

4 tbsps tomato sauce

2 tsps vegetable oil

3-4 Wurst sausages

Salt, to season

Mayonnaise, to serve

METHOD

1. Cut the potatoes into thin strips and spray with or toss in oil. Bake in the oven at 200°C (390°F, Gas Mark 6) for 20 minutes until the potatoes are golden and crunchy.

2. Meanwhile, mix the curry powder and tomato ketchup together to create a curry sauce.

3. Heat vegetable oil and fry the sausages for 5 minutes, turning to ensure they are cooked evenly.

4. Chop the sausages and smother with curry sauce Season the french fries with salt and serve with a dollop of mayonnaise.

SERVES 4 ★ PREP 10MIN ★ COOK TIME 25MIN

PORK, EGGPLANT AND RED LENTIL CURRY

INGREDIENTS

1 tbsp vegetable oil

$^1/_3$ cup (75g, 2½ oz) green curry paste

700g (1½lb) pork mince

1 large eggplant, quartered and sliced

1 cup (185g, 6oz) red lentils

1 tomatoes, chopped

2 cups (500ml, 1 pt) chicken stock

¾ cup (185ml, 6fl oz) unsweetened coconut milk

Chopped parsley, to garnish

METHOD

1. In a large frying pan or wok, heat oil over medium-high heat. Add curry paste and cook for 1 minute, stirring, until fragrant.

2. Add pork and fry for about 5 minutes or until the meat browns slightly.

3. Add eggplant and cook for 3 minutes or until it begins to soften.

4. Add lentils, tomato, stock and coconut milk and bring to a boil. Reduce heat to a simmer and cook, stirring frequently, for 15 minutes, until eggplant and lentils are tender.

5. Serve in a bowl over rice, topped with parsley.

JAPANESE CURRY RICE WITH CHEESE AND FRIED EGG

INGREDIENTS

1 cup (155g, 4oz)
short grain rice

1 tbsp olive oil

1 onion, chopped

Pinch of salt and pepper

4 cloves garlic, minced

300g (10oz) minced beef

2 cups (500ml, 1pt) water

2 Japanese curry cubes

Grated mozarella
cheese

2 eggs, fried

METHOD

1. Cook rice according to your preferred method.

2. Preheat oven to 220°C (430°F, Gas Mark 7).

3. Heat oil in a medium saucepan over medium-high heat. Add onions and salt and pepper and cook for 3 minutes until onions have softened. Add minced garlic, stir, and cook for a further 2 minutes.

4. Add beef to pan and cook, stirring constantly, for 5 minutes until browned. Add water and bring to the boil.

5. Add curry cubes to saucepan and stir until dissolved. Remove from heat.

6. Place the cooked rice on the bottom of an overproof ramekin. Pour beef curry over the rice, then cover the whole surface with grated mozzarella cheese.

7. Put ramekin into oven for 15 minutes or until cheese has fully melted and formed a golden crust.

8. Serve immediately with fried egg on top.

VIETNAMESE BEEF PHO

INGREDIENTS

Broth

2 large onions, quartered

Medium piece fresh ginger

2 cinnamon sticks

2 star anise

3 cloves

2 tsps coriander seeds

6 cups (1.5L, 50fl oz) beef stock

1 tbsp soy sauce

1 tbsp fish sauce

3 carrots, chopped

225g (8oz, ½ lb) sirloin steak

220g (8oz) dried rice noodles

Toppings

3 spring onions, sliced

2 red chillies, sliced

2 limes, wedged

60g (2oz) beansprouts

1 bunch Thai basil, torn

Hot chilli sauce

METHOD

1. Place the onion and ginger under a grill on medium heat and cook for 5 minutes each side until charred.

2. Place the cinnamon, star anise, cloves and coriander seeds in the bottom of large saucepan and dry fry, stirring, over medium-low heat for 2 minutes until aromatic.

3. Add the stock, soy sauce, fish sauce, chopped carrots, charred onions and ginger to the saucepan. Cover and bring to the boil over a medium-high heat then reduce to low and simmer for 30 minutes.

4. Meanwhile, place the beef on a plate and cover with plastic wrap. Transfer to the freezer for 15 minutes. Remove and slice across the grain into very thin slices.

5. Bring a second saucepan of water to a boil. Add rice noodles and cook according to the instructions on the packet. Strain and run under cool water to stop cooking, then divide immediately between serving bowls.

6. Arrange all the toppings on a serving dish and place on the dining table.

7. Strain the broth and discard the solids. Place the broth back over low heat and keep it just below a simmer. Heat until broth is very hot.

8. Arrange the beef in a single layer on top of noodles in each soup bowl. Ladle the hot broth over the top (it will cook the meat to medium-rare). Serve.

SPICY MAPO TOFU

INGREDIENTS

1 tbsp Sichuan peppercorns

500g (1lb 2oz) silken tofu, cubed

2 tbsps vegetable oil

200g (7oz) pork mince

2 spring onions, finely chopped, plus extra to serve

2 cloves garlic, finely chopped

2 tsp ginger, finely chopped

1 tbsp rice wine or dry sherry

2 tbsps chilli bean paste

1 cup (250ml, 8fl oz) chicken stock or water

1 tsp dark soy sauce

1 tsp white sugar

Chopped coriander leaves and sliced spring onion, to garnish

METHOD

1. Place a large frying pan on a low heat. Add peppercorns and dry fry for 1-2 minutes. Remove from the heat and whizz in a spice grinder or crush with a pestle and mortar.

2. Pour boiling water over the tofu to cover, and allow to steep for 5 minutes. Drain and set aside.

3. Place the oil in a wok or large frying pan over a high heat. Add the pork mince. Stir-fry for 1-2 minutes, stirring and turning the mince until evenly browned. Add the spring onion, garlic and ginger and stir-fry for 30 seconds.

4. Pour in the rice wine or dry sherry. Add the chilli bean paste and cook for 2 minutes until the oil turns red and beings to separate and the mixture is aromatic.

5. Add the chicken stock, bring to the boil and season with soy sauce and sugar. Ease the tofu into the wok and incorporate into the sauce without breaking it up too much. Reduce the heat and simmer for 6-7 minutes until the sauce has reduced slightly.

6. Serve garnished with sliced spring onion and chopped coriander leaves.

SEAFOOD AND FISH

Classic fish curry   110
Thai fish curry bowl   112
Hot fried clams   114
Curried prawn kebabs   115
Creamy tom yum kung   116
Nasi lemak   118
Tomato and sardine curry   120
BBQ chilli lime prawns   121
Prawn and paneer curry   122
Prawn curry fried rice   124
Vietnamese spicy fish   126
Spicy stir-fried prawns   128
Indonesian spicy snapper   129
Whole fish with yellow curry   130
Kerala fish curry   132
Easy yellow fish curry   134
Steamed fish with curry paste   135
Penang laksa   136
Easy prawn laksa   138

CLASSIC FISH CURRY

INGREDIENTS

6 fish fillets (any firm white fish), skin on

2 tbsps lemon juice

1 tsp salt

5 cloves garlic

5 dried red chillies

3 ripe tomatoes

1 tsp cumin seeds

1 tbsp vinegar

1 tsp sugar

2-3 tbsps olive or sunflower oil

1 small onion, finely chopped

1 cup (225g, 8oz) tomato paste

Fresh tomato, sliced and red chilli, sliced, to garnish

METHOD

1. Marinate the fish fillets for 10-15 minutes in the lemon juice and half a teaspoon of the salt.

2. Using a food processor or a pestle and mortar, grind together the garlic, red chillies, tomatoes, cumin seeds, remaining salt, vinegar and sugar to make a smooth paste.

3. Heat the oil in a deep frying pan. Fry the onions till light brown, approximately 5 minutes. Add the curry paste and fry for 2 minutes until aromatic. Add the tomato paste and cook for a further 2-3 minutes.

4. Add the fish fillets and enough water to almost cover the fish. Cover the pan and reduce the heat. Allow to simmer for 5-7 minutes or till the fish is tender. If the curry gets too dry, add a little more water. Cook uncovered another 2 minutes.

5. Serve in bowls with steamed rice, garnished with fresh coriander and slices of red chilli and fresh tomato.

THAI FISH CURRY BOWL

INGREDIENTS

1 pkt soba noodles

2 pieces white fish, cooked

¾ cup (185ml, 6fl oz) coconut milk

2 tbsps namya curry paste (or red curry paste)

1 tbsp fish sauce

1 tbsp ground Chinese keys (optional)

250g (9oz) fried tofu, cubed

110g (4oz) green beans, sliced

110g (4oz) white cabbage, shredded

Thai basil, to serve

METHOD

1. Cook the noodles according to the directions on the packet.

2. Mash the cooked fish in a mortar or food processor until it turns into fine fibres.

3. Heat a saucepan over medium to low heat and add ½ cup (125ml, 4fl oz) of the coconut milk and the curry paste. Let the mixture simmer until red oil starts to appear, approximately 5 minutes. Add the remaining coconut milk, fish sauce and Chinese keys, if using, and cook for a further 5 minutes. The sauce should have a thick consistency.

4. Serve in a bowl with tofu, sliced green beans, white cabbage and a garnish of Thai basil leaves.

HOT FRIED CLAMS

INGREDIENTS

700g (1½lb) clams

3 tbsps oil

2 cloves garlic, minced

2 tbsps nam prik pao
(Thai chilli paste)

6 bird's-eye chillies, bruised

Handful Thai basil leaves

½ tsp fish sauce (more to taste)

1 tsp sugar (more to taste)

Red chilli strips and Thai basil, to garnish

METHOD

1. Clean and rinse the clams well, ensuring the surface has been well scrubbed. Set aside.

2. Heat wok or large frying pan over a high heat and add oil. Stir-fry the garlic until aromatic, then add nam prik pao and bird's-eye chillies. Continue stirring for 1 minute.

3. Add clams into the wok. Stir-fry until they open, approximately 5-7 minutes, then add Thai basil leaves, fish sauce and sugar to taste. Stir once or twice before serving, garnished with strips of red chilli and Thai basil leaves.

CURRIED PRAWN KEBABS

INGREDIENTS

3 tbsps fresh lemon juice

1 tbsp soy sauce

1 tbsp Dijon mustard

2 cloves garlic, finely chopped

1 tbsp dark brown sugar

2 tsps Thai red curry paste

500g (1lb 2oz) medium raw prawns, peeled and deveined

1 capsicum, de-seeded and sliced

Rosemary, to garnish

METHOD

1. In a shallow dish, mix together the lemon juice, soy sauce, mustard, garlic, sugar and curry paste. Add prawns, stir to coat and cover. Marinate in the fridge for 1 hour.

2. Preheat barbecue to a high heat. Lightly oil the cooking grate. Thread the prawns and capsicum on to skewers.

3. Transfer the marinade to a saucepan, and boil for 2-3 minutes. Remove from the heat and transfer to the barbecue area.

4. Barbecue prawns for 3 minutes each side, or until opaque, basting occasionally with the marinade.

CREAMY TOM YUM KUNG

INGREDIENTS

2 cups (500ml, 1 pt) chicken stock

1 stalk lemongrass, sliced

Small piece galangal or ginger, very thinly sliced

6-7 kaffir lime leaves, torn

170g (6oz) fresh button or oyster mushrooms, chopped

2 tbsps nam prik pao (Thai chilli paste)

¼ cup (60ml, 2fl oz) fish sauce

4 to 5 fresh red bird's-eye chillies, crushed

24 jumbo prawns, peeled and deveined, with the head and tail sections intact

1 bunch choy sum (or other Asian green)

1 cup (250ml, 8fl oz) evapourated milk (or coconut milk)

¼ cup (5g, ¼ oz) lightly packed coriander leaves

1 lime, juiced, to serve

Fish sauce, to serve

METHOD

1. In a medium saucepan, bring the stock to a gentle boil over medium heat. Reduce the heat so that the liquid is just simmering. Add the lemongrass, galangal or ginger, and kaffir lime leaves. Next add the mushrooms and stir in the nam prik pao. Add fish sauce, followed by crushed chillies.

2. As the broth is simmering, gently drop the prawns into it. Turn up the heat a small amount to keep the broth at a steady simmer. Cook for about 1 minute, stirring occasionally, until the prawns have firmed up slightly. Add choy sum.

3. Add milk, cook until simmering again and then remove from the heat. Season soup with lime juice and fish sauce to taste. Stir in coriander leaves and serve.

NASI LEMAK

INGREDIENTS

2 cups (310g, 8oz) rice

1 x 165ml (5.6oz) can coconut milk

Pinch of salt

90g (3oz) anchovies

1 tsp belacan
(shrimp paste)

¾ cup (30g, 1oz) dried anchovies

4 shallots

1 clove garlic, peeled

8 dried chillies, deseeded

1 cup (170g, 6oz) tamarind pulp

1 cup (250ml, 8fl oz) water

¼ tsp salt

1 tbsp sugar

1 small cucumber, sliced

¾ cup (90g, 3oz) peanuts

2 hard boiled eggs, quartered

Mint and sliced chilli, to garnish

METHOD

1. Rinse rice 3 times or until water runs clear. Prepare a pan of water. Add rice, coconut milk and a pinch of salt, and bring to the boil. Simmer, covered, for 12 minutes. Drain and set aside.

2. Clean the anchovies, cut them into half and season with salt. Deep fry for 2 minutes until crispy. Set aside.

3. Place belacan, dried anchovies, shallots, garlic, and chillies in a food processor, and pulse to a rough paste.

4. Soak the tamarind pulp in hot water for 15 minutes. Squeeze occasionally to extract the flavor into the water. Drain the pulp through a sieve and retain the tamarind juice.

5. Heat some oil in a pan and fry the spice paste until fragrant. Add retained tamarind juice, salt, and sugar. Simmer on low heat until the gravy thickens. Set aside.

6. Serve steamed coconut milk rice in centre of a serving platter. Arrange sauce, anchovies, cucumber slices, peanuts and hard-boiled eggs around it. Garnish with chilli slices and sprig of mint.

SERVES 2 ★ PREP 20min ★ COOK TIME 20min

TOMATO AND SARDINE CURRY

INGREDIENTS

1 onion, chopped

1 tomato, chopped

6 garlic cloves, peeled

2 green chillies, deseeded and sliced

6 tbsp oil

½ cup (125ml, 4fl oz) fresh coconut paste

¼ tsp red chilli paste

1 tsp ground coriander

½ tsp ground turmeric

1 tsp salt

2 whole dried red chillies

10 curry leaves

¾ tsp black mustard seeds

½ cup 85g (3oz) tamarind extract

1 cup (250ml, 8fl oz) water

6 fresh sardines

METHOD

1. Using a pestle and mortar or food processor, combine onion, tomatoes, garlic and green chillies to make a paste. Set aside.

2. Heat half the oil in a frying pan over medium heat. Add coconut paste and cook for 3-4 minutes or until golden brown. Add dry spices and cook for about 3 minutes, stirring continously. Add red chilli paste and cook for 2-3 minutes until aromatic. Remove from heat and set aside.

3. Heat remaning oil in another saucepan. Add whole red chillies, curry leaves and mustard seeds. Fry until seeds splutter. Add onion paste and fry until brown.

4. Add cooked coconut paste, tamarind extract and water to the pan. Stir well and bring to a boil.

5. Reduce the heat and add sardines, then simmer for 10 minutes.

BBQ CHILLI LIME PRAWNS

INGREDIENTS

½ cup (125ml, 4fl oz) lime juice

2 tbsps fish sauce

2 tbsps chopped coriander

3 cloves garlic, finely chopped

2 small red chillies, seeds removed and sliced

1½ tsps sugar

20 large green prawns

60g (2oz) butter

2 limes, halved

Red chilli, sliced and parsley leaves, to garnish

METHOD

1. Mix the lime juice, fish sauce, coriander, garlic, chillies and sugar together in a large bowl to create a lime marinade.

2. Peel the shell from the tail portion of each prawn. Toss the prawns with the lime marinade.

3. On a hot grill cook each prawn for 2-3 minutes each side, basting liberally with butter.

4. Grill lime halves, cut side down for 3 minutes. Serve lime alongside prawns, and garnish with red chilli and parsley leaves.

PRAWN AND PANEER CURRY

INGREDIENTS

2 tbsps tomato puree

4 tbsps Greek yoghurt

1½ tbsps garam masala

1 tsp chilli powder

1 tsp garlic, crushed

1 tsp salt

2 tsps Amchur (mango) powder (or lemon juice)

1 tsp ground coriander

½ cup 120g (4oz) butter or ghee

1 tbsp oil

175g (6oz) paneer or cottage cheese, cubed

12 cooked king or tiger prawns, unpeeled

3 green chillies, chopped

Handful coriander leaves, chopped

²/₃ cup (160ml, 5fl oz) single cream

Green chilli, to garnish

METHOD

1. Mix together the tomato puree, yoghurt, garam masala, chilli powder, crushed garlic, salt, mango powder and ground coriander in bowl and set aside.

2. Melt butter or ghee with oil in heavy-based frying pan on a meduim high heat. Fry paneer cubes for 2 minutes, turning during to cook evenly. Remove from pan.

3. Add the prawns and fry for 2 minutes each side. Drain the paneer and prawns on a kitchen towel.

4. Place the spice mixture into the pan and stir-fry for 1 minute. Add the paneer and prawns.

5. Cook for a further 5-7 minutes, stirring occasionally until the prawns are cooked through.

6. Add chillies and chopped coriander and pour in cream. Cook for a further 2 minutes before serving, garnished with green chilli.

PRAWN CURRY FRIED RICE

INGREDIENTS

2 cups (310g, 8oz) jasmine rice

6 cups (1.5L, 50fl oz) water

1 tbs vegetable oil

400g (14oz) prawns, peeled and deveined

1 red capsicum, sliced

1 green capsicum, sliced

2 bunches spring onions, finely sliced

2 cloves garlic, crushed

1 tbs yellow curry paste

2 tsp fish sauce

4 lime quarters

Chopped coriander leaves, to garnish

METHOD

1   Rinse the rice with water through a sieve three times or until the water runs clear. Place the rice and water in a medium saucepan over a high heat and bring to the boil. Reduce the heat to medium and simmer uncovered for 10-12 minutes or until the rice is soft. Drain well.

2.   Meanwhile, heat the vegetable oil in a wok or large frying pan over a high heat. Add the prawns and cook, turning, for 1-2 minutes or until they just turn opaque. Remove from the pan and set aside. Add the red and green capsicum and the white parts of the spring onion.

3.   Stir-fry for 2-3 minutes or until just tender. Add in the garlic, yellow curry paste and fish sauce and cook, stirring, for 1 minute or until fragrant. Add the rice, prawns and the green parts of the spring onion and stir until everything is evenly coated in the paste. Squeeze in the juice of the lime wedges. Remove from the heat.

4.   To serve, divide the fried rice between bowls and garnish with chopped coriander.

VIETNAMESE SPICY FISH

INGREDIENTS

Caramel sauce

¼ cup (60ml, 2fl oz) water

2 tbsps of sugar

Curry

6 fish pieces (meaty fish such as mackerel)

4 tbsps fish sauce

3 tbsps brown sugar

1 tbsp black pepper

2 tbsps minced garlic

2 tbsps minced shallots

Oil, for frying

Coconut water, as required

Fresh coriander leaves and sliced spring onions, to garnish

METHOD

1. Bring the water to the boil and add the sugar. Keep at a rolling simmer, stirring constantly until the syrup is dark brown but not burnt. Set caramel sauce aside.

2. Rinse fish steaks and pat dry. Prepare a marinade with fish sauce, sugar, pepper, garlic and shallots. Add fish, cover and marinate in a cool place for 1 hour.

3. Heat oil in a large casserole over medium-high heat and add the marinated fish. Sear and brown on one side for 2-3 minutes before searing the other side for 2-3 minutes. Add 3 tablespoons of the caramel sauce and just enough coconut water to reach the level of the fish steaks.

4. Cover and reduce heat to medium-low. Allow to simmer for 25 min, checking occasionally that the sauce has not reduced too much. Add more coconut juice or caramel sauce if needed. Taste and adjust for flavour with fish sauce or sugar.

5. Remove from the heat and garnish with spring onions and fresh coriander.

SPICY STIR-FRIED PRAWNS

INGREDIENTS

1 tbsp oil

1 tbsp Thai red curry paste

330g (12oz) prawns, peeled and deveined

½ cup (125ml, 4fl oz) chicken stock or vegetable stock

1 tsp fish sauce

½ tsp sugar

1 cup (15g, ½ oz) fresh basil leaves

4 long red chillies (optional)

METHOD

1. Heat oil in the pan over the medium heat and fry the curry paste until aromatic.

2. Add prawns and stir for 3 minutes or until prawns turn opaque.

3. Add chicken stock, fish sauce and sugar to taste. Cook further for 1 minute or so or until the prawns are cooked thoroughly.

4. Add fresh basil and red chillies, if using, and stir. Serve hot with rice and salad.

INDONESIAN SPICY SNAPPER

INGREDIENTS

Curry paste

5 Asian shallots, peeled

4 red chillies, stemmed

4 garlic cloves

Small piece ginger, thinly sliced

½ tsp ground turmeric

¾ tsp ground coriander

4 macadamia nuts

Curry

2 whole red snapper sliced crosswise (head and tails discarded)

2 tsps fresh lime juice

3 tbsps vegetable oil

6 kaffir lime leaves

2 red chillies, sliced

1 stalk lemongrass, crushed

1 bay leaf

½ cup (125ml, 4fl oz) coconut milk

1½ tbsps tamarind concentrate

1 spring onion, finely sliced

3 tbsps coconut cream

1 tbsp palm sugar, grated

Salt, to taste

METHOD

1. Place shallots, chillies, garlic, ginger, turmeric, coriander, nuts, salt, and 2 tablespoons water in food processor and blend to a smooth paste. Set aside the curry paste.

2. Rub fish with lime juice and season with salt. Leave to marinate for 10 minutes.

3. Heat oil in a pan over medium-high heat. Add curry paste, kaffir lime leaves, chillies, lemongrass, and bay leaf. Cook, stirring constantly, for 4-5 minutes or until aromatic.

4. Stir in coconut milk and 1¼ (310ml, 10fl oz) cups water and bring to boil. Reduce heat to medium and cook, stirring occasionally, for 5 minutes.

5. Add tamarind and spring onion and stir. Add fish and cook until fish is cooked but not falling apart, 4–6 minutes. Stir in coconut cream and palm sugar and season with salt.

WHOLE FISH WITH YELLOW CURRY

INGREDIENTS

3 tbsps coconut oil

1 tbsp yellow curry paste

1 sprig fresh curry leaves

1 star anise

2 whole cloves

1 cinnamon stick

¾ cup (200ml, 7fl oz) fish stock

1¼ cups (300ml, 10fl oz) coconut milk

2 tbsps palm sugar, grated

4 kaffir lime leaves

2 tbsps tamarind water or puree

2 tbsps coconut cream

Salt, to taste

1 whole firm white fish (such as kingfish)

Iceberg lettuce, red chilli strips and shredded kaffir lime leaves to garnish

METHOD

1. Heat 1 tablespoon coconut oil in a wok or large frying pan until it shimmers. Fry curry paste and curry leaves until fragrant and the paste begins to split. Then add star anise, cloves and cinnamon, and cook for 1 minute until the spices are aromatic. Stir in fish stock, coconut milk, palm sugar and kaffir lime leaves.

2. Reduce the heat to a simmer and cook for 10-15 minutes until flavours intensify. Add tamarind water and coconut cream. Add salt to taste. Strain the sauce.

3. Heat 2 tablespoons coconut oil in a frying pan over a medium-high heat, place fish skin-side down and apply pressure to ensure it cooks evenly. Cook for 4 minutes or until skin is crisp. Turn over and cook for a further 3 minutes until just cooked. Remove from frying pan and rest.

4. To serve, place the fish on a bed of iceberg lettuce and garnish with red chill strips and shredded kaffir lime leaves.

KERALA FISH CURRY

INGREDIENTS

1½ kg (3lb 5oz) firm white fish, cut into large cubes

Salt

2 tsps turmeric, divided

1 tbsp vegetable oil

2 medium onions, sliced

2 long red chillies, deseeded and sliced

Medium piece ginger, cut into thin strips

Pinch of ground cumin

2 Thai eggplants, chopped

1 x 400ml (14fl oz) can coconut milk

1 tbsp tamarind paste

1 tbsp fish stock concentrate

Boiling water, as needed

Curry leaves, to garnish

METHOD

1. Rub fish pieces with a salt and 1 teaspoon turmeric. Set aside.

2. Heat the oil in a large, shallow frying pan and add the onion and cook for 5 minutes, stirring, until the onion has softened.

3. Add chilli, remaining teaspoon of turmeric and cumin. Fry for a further 2 minutes. Add the Thai eggplant and fry for 5 minutes.

4. Pour the coconut milk into a measuring jug. Add tamarind paste and the fish stock concentrate, and then add boiling water as needed to bring the liquid up to the litre (4 cups, 2pt) mark. Pour it into the pan and cook gently for 5 minutes, stirring occasionally, until eggplant is tender.

5. When you are almost ready to eat, add the fish to the hot sauce and heat for 5 minutes, until cooked through. Garnish with curry leaves.

EASY YELLOW FISH CURRY

INGREDIENTS

3 tsps vegetable oil

2 red onions, cut into wedges

½ cup (125ml, 4fl oz) Thai yellow curry paste

1 cup (270ml, 9fl oz) coconut cream

750g (1½lb) white fish fillets, cut into pieces

2 tbsps lime juice

1 tbsp brown sugar

2 tsps fish sauce

Coriander leaves, to garnish

METHOD

1. Heat the oil in a wok or large frying pan over a medium-high heat. Add onion and stir-fry for 2 mins or until lightly browned. Add curry paste and stir-fry for 1 minute or until aromatic.

2. Stir in coconut cream and bring to the boil. Reduce heat to medium-low. Add fish and cook, gently, stirring occasionally, for 5 minutes or until the fish is just cooked through. Remove from heat. Stir in lime juice, sugar and fish sauce. Taste and add more lime juice, sugar or fish sauce, if desired.

3. Serve in bowls garnished with coriander leaves.

STEAMED FISH WITH CURRY PASTE

INGREDIENTS

1 fresh banana leaf

2 snapper fillets

1 tbsp Thai red curry paste

2 tbsps coconut cream

Medium piece ginger, finely sliced

8 kaffir lime leaves, shredded

2 tbsps coriander, chopped

Dressing

2 tbsps fish sauce

2 limes, juiced

2 tbsps sweet chilli sauce

METHOD

1. Preheat the oven to 180°C (350°F, Gas Mark 4). Wash banana leaf and cut pieces large enough to enclose the fish.

2. Cut 2 slashes in the thickest part of the flesh. Place square of foil on the banana leaf, then top with the fish. Smear fish with curry paste, then spoon over the coconut cream. Scatter with ginger, kaffir lime leaves and coriander, then enclose the fish in the leaf and tie the ends with kitchen string.

3. Place the parcel in a roasting pan and bake for 40 minutes or until cooked through.

4. Meanwhile, to prepare the dressing, combine fish sauce, lime juice and sweet chilli sauce in small bowl.

5 Spoon dressing over fish to serve.

PENANG LAKSA

INGREDIENTS

450g (1lb) mackerel

8 cups (2L, 4pt) water

5 pieces peeled tamarind

12 dried red chillies, de-seeded

5 fresh red chillies, de-seeded

8 small Asian shallots

2 tsps belacan (shrimp paste)

1 stalk lemongrass, pale part only

Oil for frying

30g (1oz) block pressed tamarind, roughly chopped

Salt, to taste

Sugar, to taste

Fish sauce, to taste

1 pkt dried laksa noodles

1 lettuce, shredded, to garnish

Red onion, thinly sliced, to garnish

METHOD

1. Clean and scale the fish, if required. Bring 8 cups of water to boil in a large saucepan. Add the fish and boil for 10 minutes. Strain, retaining the fish stock in the saucepan. Transfer cooked fish to a bowl to cool.

2. Add the tamarind pieces to the fish stock and bring to a simmer.

3. With wet hands, pick the flesh of the fish and discard the bones. Break fish meat into small pieces and place back in the stock. Cover and redude heat to low.

4. In a food processor or spice grinder, grind the chillies, shallots, shrimp paste and lemongrass to a fine paste.

5. Place chopped tamarind block in 1 cup (250ml, 8fl oz) measuring cup and almost fill with boiling water. Allow to soak for 15 minutes.

6. Heat oil in a large pan or wok and add the spice paste. Fry for 5 minutes or until fragrant. Add the spice paste to the fish stock.

7. Strain the tamarind. Add the tamarind juice to the stock.

8. Taste and season with salt, sugar and fish sauce as required.

9. Prepare the noodles according to the instructions on the packet.

10. Place cooked noodles in a large serving bowl and garnish with lettuce and red onion. Pour the soup stock over the top and serve.

EASY PRAWN LAKSA

INGREDIENTS

2 tsps olive oil

1 x 230g (8oz) jar
laksa paste

2 cups (500ml, 1 pt)
chicken stock

1 x 400ml (14fl oz)
can coconut milk

750g (1½ lb) green
prawns, peeled

120g (4¼ oz) snow
peas, whole

1 tsp fish sauce

200g (7oz) rice noodles

½ cup (10g, ½ oz)
coriander leaves

Handful of bean sprouts

Thinly sliced fresh
red chilli (optional) and
lime wedges, to garnish

METHOD

1. Heat the oil in a wok over medium heat. Add the laksa paste and cook, stirring, for 2 minutes. Add the stock and coconut milk, and stir to combine.

2. Reduce the heat, bringing the coconut milk mixture to a simmer. Add the prawns and snow peas. Cook for 3-4 minutes or until the prawns are just cooked through. Stir in the fish sauce.

3. Meanwhile, place the noodles in a large heatproof bowl. Add enough boiling water to cover. Set aside for 10 minutes or until soft. Drain.

4. Divide the noodles among serving bowls. Pour over the coconut milk mixture and top with the coriander, bean sprouts, lime wedges and chilli, if using.

BEANS
AND
PULSES

Green cinnamon lentils 142

Spicy vegan curry burgers 144

Chilli lentil soup 146

Roasted spicy chickpeas 148

Chickpea spinach curry 149

Chickpea channa masala 150

Cashew and red bean curry 152

Kidney bean curry 154

South African bean curry 155

Red lentil Indian soup 156

Curried lentil patties 158

Traditional dahl makhani 160

Green lentil curry 162

Dahl tadka 163

Lentil and potato crepes 164

Classic yellow dahl 166

Spinach and lentil soup 168

Black chickpeas curry 169

GREEN CINNAMON LENTILS

INGREDIENTS

2 tbsps olive oil

1 small onion, diced

1 tbsp fresh ginger, minced

2 garlic cloves, minced

2 fresh jalapeño peppers, diced (optional)

1 tsp ground cumin

1 tbsp curry powder

1 tsp salt

2½ cups (625ml, 20fl oz) water

1 cup (185g, 6oz) dried green lentils

2 medium tomatoes, diced

1 tsp ground cinnamon

Parsley, to garnish

METHOD

1. Heat oil in a large saucepan over medium-high heat. Add onions and cook until soft and golden, approximately 5 minutes. Add ginger, garlic and jalapeños and cook for 1 further minute.

2. Add cumin, curry powder, and salt and cook for 1 further minute.

3. Stir in water and lentils and bring the mixture to a boil. Reduce to a simmer and cook uncovered for 15 minutes, allowing most of the moisture to evapourate.

4. Add tomatoes and cinnamon and simmer covered for 10-15 more minutes until the lentils are tender.

SPICY VEGAN CURRY BURGERS

INGREDIENTS

2 cups (500ml, 1pt)
vegetable stock

1 cup (185g, 6oz) millet

1 sweet potato, chopped

1 medium onion, chopped

3 cloves garlic

1 x 425g (15oz) can
chickpeas

2 tbsps olive oil

3 tbsps coriander
leaves, chopped

¼ cup (40g, 1½ oz)
dried apricots, chopped

2 tbsp almonds, chopped

½ preserved lemon

1 tsp turmeric

2 tsps ground cumin

2 tsps ground coriander

½ tsp ground ginger

⅛ tsp ground cinnamon

2 tsps harissa (or chilli
paste)

3 eggs

½ cup (60g, 2oz)
breadcrumbs

Hamburger buns, lettuce,
onion, avocado, tomato
to serve

METHOD

1. Bring the vegetable stock to a boil in a saucepan and add the millet. Reduce the heat to medium, cover and simmer for 15 minutes. Turn off the heat and let sit for 10 minutes.

2. Place sweet potato, onion and garlic in a food processor and pulse until finely chopped. Transfer to a bowl. Then pulse the chickpeas until finely chopped and transfer to the same bowl.

3. Heat oil in a frying pan over medium-high heat and cook the sweet potato mixture and chickpeas until soft, approximately 5-7 minutes. Add the coriander, apricots, almonds, preserved lemon, spices and harissa. Cook for another 2 minutes. Remove from heat and cool.

4. Combine the sweet potato and chickpea mixture with the millet and breadcrumbs. Add the eggs and stir until well combined.

5. Form balls of the mixture into patties between your hands. When finished cover patties with plastic wrap and refrigerate for 3-4 hours.

6. Heat oil in a large frying pan over medium-high heat. When hot, add the patties and cook until browned, about 4-5 minutes on each side.

7. Place the patties on hamburger buns with lettuce, onion, avocado and tomato.

CHILLI LENTIL SOUP

INGREDIENTS

1½ cups (275g, 9oz)
brown lentils

1 tbsp olive oil or ghee

1 onion, chopped

3 garlic cloves, crushed

2 tsps ground cumin

2 tsps ground coriander

2 tsps paprika

1 tsp chilli powder

2 red capsicums, chopped

2 carrots, diced

1 celery stick, chopped

4 cups (1L, 2pt)
vegetable stock

2 x 400g (14oz) cans
chopped tomatoes

Salt and pepper,
to taste

Basil leaves,
to garnish

METHOD

1. Rinse the lentils under cold water, removing any dirt.

2. Place oil or ghee in a wok or large frying pan over medium-low heat. Add the onions and garlic and slowly cook until soft, approximately 7-10 minutes.

3. Add the ground spices and chilli and cook until fragrant, approximately 2 minutes.

4. Add the capsicum, carrots and celery and cook, stirring, for 2-3 minutes.

5. Add the lentils, stock, tomatoes, salt and pepper and cook, covered, on a low heat for 45 minutes or until the lentils are tender.

6. Serve, garnished with basil leaves.

ROASTED SPICY CHICKPEAS

INGREDIENTS

1 x 400g (14oz) can chickpeas, drained, rinsed

½ tsp salt

2 tsps sweet paprika

1½ tsps ground cumin

2 tsps mild curry powder

METHOD

1. Preheat oven to 170°C (340°F, Gas Mark 4) and line a baking tray with greaseproof paper.

2. Place chickpeas on prepared tray. Sieve the spices over the top and toss to coat. Ensure even coating of the chickpeas.

3. Roast chickpeas for 1 hour or until golden and crispy. Then cool chickpeas on baking tray.

4. Store in an airtight container, at room temperature, for up to 2 days.

CHICKPEA SPINACH CURRY

METHOD

1. Place the onion, garlic, ginger and tomatoes in a food processor or blender and puree to form a smooth curry paste.

2. In a small bowl, mix together toasted sesame seeds and chopped cashew nuts. Set aside.

3. Heat oil in a large pan on a medium-high heat. Add the spices, fry for 1 minute and then add curry paste and Vegemite. Allow the paste and yeast to bubble together for 2 mins.

4. Next add the lentils and coconut cream. Cook until lentils are tender, approximately 15 minutes. Stir in chickpeas and spinach, and allow to warm through, approximately 3 minutes.

5. When ready to serve, add lemon juice and mix through with the sesame and cashew mixture.

INGREDIENTS

1 onion, chopped

2 garlic cloves, chopped

Medium piece ginger, grated

6 tomatoes

1 tbsp toasted sesame seeds

1 tbsp cashew nuts, chopped

½ tbsp oil

1 tsp ground cumin

2 tsps ground coriander

1 tsp turmeric

Pinch of chilli flakes

1 tsp Vegemite (or other yeast-extract spread)

4 tbsps red lentils

6 tbsps coconut cream

1 x 400g (14oz) can chickpeas, drained

1 bunch spinach, leaves picked

1 lemon, juiced

CHICKPEA CHANNA MASALA

INGREDIENTS

2 tbsps ground coriander

1 tbsp ground cumin

1 tsp turmeric

½ tsp pepper

1 tsp chilli powder
(optional)

2 garlic cloves, crushed

Small piece ginger,
chopped

2½ tbsps lemon juice

2 tbsps olive oil

1 meduim onion, chopped

2 tbsps tomato paste

1 medium tomato,
chopped

2 x 400g (14oz) cans
chickpeas

1 cup (250ml, 8fl oz)
vegetable stock

Coriander sprig, to garnish

METHOD

1. Place coriander, cumin, turmeric, pepper, chilli (if using), garlic, ginger and lemon juice in a bowl and mix to form a paste. Set spice paste aside.

2. Heat 1 tablespoon of oil in a large saucepan over medium-high heat. Add the onion and cook, stirring, for 5-7 minutes, or until golden.

3. Reduce heat to medium. Add spice paste. Cook for 1 minute to release spices. Add tomato paste, tomato, chickpeas and stock. Bring to the boil. Reduce heat to low.

4. Cook, uncovered, for a further 15 minutes, or until sauce has reduced and thickened slightly.

5. Serve in bowls with naan bread and garnish with coriander leaves.

CASHEW AND RED BEAN CURRY

INGREDIENTS

Olive oil, for frying

1 bunch spinach leaves, washed and roughly chopped

3 cups (750ml, 24fl oz) passata

1 cup (250ml, 8fl oz) cashew butter

1 x 400g (14 oz) can kidney beans

2 tomatoes, chopped

½ tsp salt

½ tsp pepper

1 tsp curry powder

½ tsp ground cardamom

Hot water, as required

50g (2oz) cashew nuts

METHOD

1. Heat olive oil in a large heavy-based saucepan and add the chopped spinach. Fry for 2-3 minutes.

2. Add passata and cashew butter. Mix well and heat until nearly boiling on medium heat.

3. Reduce the heat. Add beans, tomatoes, salt, pepper, curry powder and cardamom. Keep the stew cooking at a gentle simmer for 15 minutes until spices have fully absorbed. Add a little hot water if needed to thin the sauce.

4. In a small saucepan, dry roast cashew nuts for 3-4 minutes until they brown lightly. Remove from heat.

5. Serve in a bowl sprinkled with toasted cashews.

SERVES 4 ★ PREP 20MIN ★ COOK TIME 25MIN

KIDNEY BEAN CURRY

INGREDIENTS

Oil, for cooking

1 onion, diced

3 cloves garlic, crushed

Small piece ginger, peeled and grated

2 green bird's-eye chilli finely chopped

1½ cups (375ml, 13fl oz) crushed tomatoes and juices, or passata

1 tbsp ground coriander

1 tbsp ground cumin

1½ tsps garam masala

2 x 400g (14oz) cans red kidney beans, drained and rinsed

¼ cup (60ml, 2fl oz) vegetable stock

Hot water, as required

Salt and pepper, to taste

Fresh mint and tomato slices, to garnish

METHOD

1. Heat the oil in a heavy-based pot and add the onions. Fry over a medium-high heat, until the onions are soft and golden, approximately 7 minutes.

2. Add the garlic, ginger and chillies, and fry together until fragrant.

3. Add tomatoes, ground coriander, cumin and garam masala. Season with a little salt. Turn down the heat and cook, stirring every so often until the masala starts reducing, and the oil starts separating from it, approximately 7 to 10 minutes

4. Add the kidney beans and the stock. Simmer for a few more minutes, until the beans are heated through. Add a little more hot water if the sauce is too thick.

5. Taste, season and serve, garnished with fresh mint leaves and tomato slices.

SOUTH AFRICAN BEAN CURRY

INGREDIENTS

6 dried apricots

12 prunes, pitted

½ cup (80g, 3oz) sultanas or raisins

1½ cups (375ml, 13fl oz) boiling water

2 tbsps sunflower oil

2 onions, finely chopped

4 cloves garlic, finely chopped

1-2 green chillies (to taste), finely chopped

Small piece ginger, finely chopped

1 green capsicum, finely chopped

1 tsp ground cumin

1 tsp ground coriander

1 tsp fennel seeds

1 cinnamon stick

1 x 400g (14oz) can red kidney beans

3 cups (465g, 12oz) plain boiled rice

¼ cup (30g, 1oz) toasted peanuts, chopped

1 ripe banana, sliced

METHOD

1. Place the dried fruit in a small saucepan and cover with boiling water. Cover the pot and bring back to the boil. Reduce the heat to a simmer and cook for about 20 minutes, until the fruit is plump. Do not drain.

2. Meanwhile, heat a large saucepan over a medium heat and add oil. Fry the onions until golden. Add the garlic, chillies, ginger, capsicum and all the spices. Cook, stirring, until fragrant, about 1-2 minutes, then add the kidney beans and season with salt to taste.

3. Pour in the fruit with the cooking water. Stir and bring to the boil, then simmer for about 30 minutes, stirring frequently. Taste for seasoning.

4. Serve the curry mixed through the boiled rice, sprinkled with peanuts and a few slices of banana.

RED LENTIL INDIAN SOUP

INGREDIENTS

1½ cups (275g, 9oz) red lentils, rinsed

4 cups (1L, 2 pt) vegetable stock

2 tomatoes, diced

1 tsp salt

1 tbsp olive oil

1 tsp mustard seeds

1 tsp cumin seeds

2 green chillies, chopped

1 tsp chopped garlic

1 tsp chopped fresh ginger

1 onion, finely chopped

½ tsp turmeric

¼ tsp cayenne pepper

¼ tsp asafoetida (optional)

2 tsps ground coriander

Pinch of ground cinnamon

Pinch of ground cloves

1 lime, juiced

Salt, to taste

Coriander, to garnish

METHOD

1. Place the rinsed lentils, vegetable stock, tomatoes, and salt in a large, heavy-based pot.

2. Heat the oil in a small frying pan over a high heat and add the mustard and cumin seeds. Fry for 20 second until the mustard seeds begin to pop. Reduce the heat to medium-high and add the chillies, garlic and ginger. Fry for a further 20 seconds. Add the onion and fry until soft and golden brown, about 5-7 minutes. Add the turmeric, cayenne, asafoetida, if using, coriander, cinnamon and cloves and stir to combine.

3. Transfer the contents of the frying pan into the stock pot. Stir to combine and bring to a boil. Reduce the heat, cover, and simmer, stirring occasionally, for about 20 minutes, or until the lentils are done and the soup is a thick consistency.

4. Before serving, gradually add the lime juice, to taste. Add more salt as needed. Serve sprinkled with fresh coriander.

SERVES 6 ★ PREP 25MIN (PLUS FREEZING) ★ COOK TIME 10MIN

CURRIED LENTIL PATTIES

INGREDIENTS

1 sweet potato, sliced

2 x 400g (14oz) cans lentils, drained

2 tbsps olive oil

4 spring onions, sliced

1 tbsp mild curry powder

Medium piece ginger, finely grated

2 zucchini, coarsely grated

½ cup (60g, 2oz) dried breadcrumbs

METHOD

1. Cook sweet potato in a large saucepan of boiling water until just tender. Drain and return to the pan. Mash until smooth. Add lentils and mash again until combined.

2. Meanwhile, heat half the oil in a frying pan over a medium-high heat. Add the spring onion and cook, stirring, for 3 minutes or until softened. Add curry powder and ginger. Cook, stirring, for 1 minute or until fragrant. Remove from pan.

3. Combine onion mixture and zucchini with sweet potato mixture. Season with salt and pepper.

4. Prepare two plates and cover one with the breadcrumbs. Shape mixture into thick patties using hands. Coat patties in breadcrumbs and transfer coated patties to the second plate. Cover in cling wrap and place in freezer for 15 minutes.

5. Heat the remaining oil in a large frying pan over a medium heat. Cook patties, in batches, for 3 to 4 minutes each side or until crispy and heated through. Serve.

TRADITIONAL DAHL MAKHANI

INGREDIENTS

1 cup (200g, 7oz)
dried whole black lentils

½ cup (55g, 2oz)
dried kidney beans

8 cups (2L, 4pt)
vegetable stock

3 tbsps ghee or oil

2 large onions, chopped

6 cloves garlic, grated

Small piece ginger, grated

1 bay leaf

1 cinnamon stick

2 green cardamom pods

2 cloves

1-2 hot red chillies
(to taste)

¼ tsp pepper

1½ tbsps garam masala

1 tsp each ground
coriander, cumin, chilli
powder, sweet paprika

1 tsp salt

1 x 400g (14oz) can
diced tomatoes

170g (6oz) tomato paste

4 tbsps (60g, 2oz) butter

½ cup (125ml, 4fl oz)
heavy cream

METHOD

1. Soak the black lentils and kidney beans in a large bowl for 8 hours or overnight. Rinse and drain.

2. Add the lentils, beans and stock to a large pot and bring to a boil. Cover the pot, turn heat down to simmer, and cook for 1 hour, stirring occasionally.

3. Meanwhile, heat the ghee or oil in a large frying pan over medium-high heat. Add the onion and cook until caramelised, about 15 minutes, stirring occasionally.

4. Reduce the heat to medium and add the garlic and ginger. Cook for 1 minute, stirring constantly.

5. Add the bay leaf, cinnamon stick, cardamom pods, cloves, red chillies, black pepper and all of the ground spices. Cook until fragrant, about 1 minute, stirring constantly. Remove from heat.

6. Stir the onion/spice mixture, salt, diced tomatoes, and tomato paste into the lentils and beans.

7. Gently simmer until the sauce has thickened and the lentils and beans are tender, about 45 minutes to 1 hour, stirring frequently. Cover the pot if the sauce is too thick.

8. When ready to eat, turn off the heat and stir in the butter and cream. Garnish with coriander leaves and serve.

GREEN LENTIL CURRY

INGREDIENTS

1 tsp coconut oil

1 large onion, finely chopped

6 garlic cloves, crushed

1 tsp brown mustard seeds

1 tsp turmeric

½ tsp ground coriander

1 tsp curry powder

1 tsp cumin

1¼ tsps salt

1 x 400ml (14fl oz) can coconut milk

²/₃ cup (150g, 5oz) tomato paste

3 cups (750ml, 24fl oz) boiling water

1 cup (200g, 7oz) uncooked green lentils, rinsed

Chopped coriander, to garnish

METHOD

1. Heat oil in a saucepan on low-medium heat. Add onion and cook, stirring occasionally, until golden brown, approximately 5 minutes. Add garlic and fry for 1-2 minutes until the strong aroma disappears. Next add the brown mustard seeds and cook for a minute or two until they pop. Then add turmeric, coriander, curry powder, cumin and salt and cook for another 30 seconds, stirring frequently.

2. Pour in the coconut milk, tomato paste, water and lentils and stir to combine. Bring to a boil, cover and cook on a low heat for 45 minutes.

3. Season to taste before serving garnished with chopped coriander.

DAHL TADKA

INGREDIENTS

1 cup (185g, 6oz) yellow split peas, uncooked

2 cups (500ml, 1pt) vegetable stock (or water)

1 tsp turmeric

¼ tsp cayenne

½ tsp salt

1 tbsp butter or ghee

1 onion, diced

1½ tsps cumin, whole seeds or ground

2 whole cloves

Salt and pepper, to taste

Chopped coriander, to garnish

METHOD

1. Place the peas and water or vegetable stock into a large pot and bring to a slow simmer. Add the turmeric, cayenne and salt, and cover. Cook for at least 20 minutes, stirring occasionally.

2. In a large frying pan, heat the butter or ghee. Add the onion, cumin and cloves and cook for 5-6 minutes until onion is soft. Add the onion and spice mix to the split peas, and simmer for at least 5 more minutes.

3. Season to taste before serving garnished with chopped coriander.

LENTIL AND POTATO CREPES

INGREDIENTS

1½ cups (275g, 9oz)
red lentils, rinsed

Butter or ghee, for frying

½ onion, diced

2 tbsps red curry paste

½ tbsp garam masala

1 tsp curry powder

½ tsp turmeric

Pinch of cayenne

1 tsp sugar

1 tsp garlic, minced

1 tsp ginger, minced

1 large potato, diced

1 x 400ml (14fl oz)
can tomato puree

¼ cup (60ml, 2fl oz)
coconut milk or cream

4 crepes, for serving

Chopped coriander leaves,
to garnish

METHOD

1. Place a saucepan of salted water over a high heat and bring to the boil. Add lentils and cook for 40 minutes or until soft and tender. Drain and set aside.

2. Melt butter or ghee in a large saucepan over medium-high heat. Add onion and saute for 3 minutes until fragrant and golden. Add the curry paste, garam masala, curry powder, turmeric, cayenne, sugar, garlic and ginger and stir-fry for 1-2 minutes. Add potato and tomato puree and stir to combine. Simmer for 2-3 minutes.

3. Add lentils and coconut milk or cream. Stir to combine and simmer for 20 minutes until soft and flavoursome.

4. Serve stuffed in a crepe and garnished with coriander.

SERVES 4 ★ PREP 15min ★ COOK TIME 40min

CLASSIC YELLOW DAHL

INGREDIENTS

1½ cups (275g, 9oz)
yellow lentils

1 tbsp vegetable oil

2 tsps black mustard seeds

1 tsp asafoetida

1 onion, thinly sliced

1 habanero or milder chilli,
to taste (optional)

2-3 garlic cloves

2½ tsps ground cumin

1 tsp garam masala

2-3 bay leaves

1 tomato, skinned and diced

5 cups (1.25L, 42fl oz)
vegetable stock

2 tbsps ginger, grated

2 tsps turmeric

½ lemon, juiced

Coriander leaves, to garnish

METHOD

1. Rinse the lentils and remove any grit or lentils that float.

2. Heat the oil in a small saucepan on a medium-high heat. When hot, add the mustard seeds and asafoetida. When the mustard seeds start to pop, add the onion and cook until softened, approximately 5 minutes. Add the chilli and garlic. Cook for a further 1 minute. Add cumin, garam masala, bay leaves and tomato. Cook for another 2-3 minutes.

3. Place the vegetable stock in a large saucepan. Add the lentils along with the ginger and turmeric. Boil for approximately 20 minutes until just tender. If you have a stick blender, place in the pan and whizz for 5-10 seconds to create an uneven consistency, or remove one cup of the lentils from the pan and puree in a blender before returning to the pan. The dahl should have a good texture with some full lentils and some thick sauce.

4. Add the spiced onion mixture to the pot of lentils, adjusting for seasoning if necessary. Cook over a medium-low heat for another 15-20 minutes.

5. Squeeze over lemon juice before serving in bowls garnished with coriander leaves.

SPINACH AND LENTIL SOUP

INGREDIENTS

2 tbsps olive oil

1 onion, chopped

2 stalks of celery, sliced

2 carrots, diced

3 cloves garlic, minced

1 tbsp curry powder

1 tbsp fresh ginger, minced

1 tsp ground cumin

1 bay leaf

¼ tsp chilli powder

2½ cups (460g, 1lb 11oz) dried lentils

175g (6oz) spinach leaves

½ cup (20g, ¾ oz) chopped coriander

METHOD

1. Heat the oil in heavy saucepan and fry onions, celery, carrot and garlic until golden, approximately 10 minutes.

2. Stir in all spices and add 8 cups (2L, 4pt) of water and lentils.

3. Reduce the heat and cook until lentils are tender, approximately 25 minutes.

4. Add the spinach and coriander and cook until wilted, about 5 minutes.

5. Season with salt and pepper.

SERVES 2 ★ PREP 10MIN (PLUS SOAKING) ★ COOK TIME 30MIN

BLACK CHICKPEA CURRY

INGREDIENTS

1 cup (185g, 6oz) black chickpeas

1 onion, minced

1½ tbsps oil

1 tsp cumin seeds

½ cup (110g, 4oz) tomato puree

Small piece ginger, grated

3 cloves garlic, grated

2 green chillies, chopped

2 long red chillies, whole

1 tsp ground turmeric

2 tsp red chilli powder

1 tbsp ground coriander

½ tsp ground chole masala (or garam masala)

1 stem curry leaves

1 tbsp lemon juice

METHOD

1. Soak the chickpeas in water for 8 hours or overnight.

2. Put the onion in a pressure cooker and cook for 10 minutes, until caramelised.

3. Add oil, cumin seeds and tomato puree and cook for 3 minutes.

4. Add grated ginger, garlic, chopped green chillies and whole red chillies. Cook for a further 3 minutes.

5. Put the chickpeas in the pressure cooker along with 1½ cups (375ml, 13fl oz) of the soaking water. Add all spices and curry leaves to the pressure cooker and stir to combine. Simmer for 3 minutes to allow the spices to infuse.

6. Close the lid of pressure cooker and cook for 20 minutes.

7. Before serving add lemon juice to the curry.

VEGETABLES

Spinach paneer butter masala   172

Chettinad egg curry   174

Potatoes with mustard seeds   176

Paneer butter curry   178

Mixed vegetable curry   179

Cauliflower kofta curry   180

Dry curried tofu   182

Peanut and spinach curry   184

Jackfruit curry   186

Curry roasted cauliflower   187

Cocktail samosas   188

Tofu, green bean and spinach curry   190

Singapore curry noodle   192

Easy okra with tomatoes   193

Curried cauliflower fritters   194

Broccoli, cashew nut and kale curry   196

Spicy salad of curried rice balls   198

Curried eggs   200

Potato and pea curry   202

Easy curry puffs   203

Okra masala curry   204

Jamaican pumpkin and pineapple curry   206

Simple potato curry   208

Sweet pineapple curry   210

Mango curry   211

Easy palak paneer   212

Tomato eggplant curry with millet   214

Spicy Japanese tofu with enoki mushrooms   216

Crispy potato bhajias   218

SPINACH PANEER BUTTER MASALA

INGREDIENTS

20 cashew nuts, roughly chopped

5-6 medium tomatoes (or use 1 x 400g/14oz can chopped tomatoes)

1 bay leaf

3 tbsp butter

1 tbsp oil

250g (9oz) paneer, cubed

Small piece ginger, julienned

½ tsp ground mace (or nutmeg)

2-3 green chillies, slit lengthwise

½ tsp garam masala

½ tsp chilli powder

1 tbsp sugar

Salt, to taste

1 bunch spinach, finely chopped

3 tbsps cream

METHOD

1. Soak the cashew nuts in warm water for 45 minutes. Remove from water and blend into a paste using a food processor or blender.

2. Boil the tomatoes in salted hot water with bay leaf for 5 minutes. Remove tomatoes and allow to cool. Peel the skin from the tomatoes. Chop and blend them to a smooth puree. (Replace this step with canned tomatoes, if using).

3. Heat pan on medium-high heat with 1 tablespoon butter and oil. Fry the paneer, turning, until golden. Remove from pan and set aside.

4. In the same pan add little more butter plus a little oil. Reduce heat to low and fry ginger and mace (or nutmeg) for 1 minute. Add chillies and fry for 20 seconds.

5. Add the cashew paste and fry, stirring, until the paste thickens. Add the tomato puree. Simmer and keep stirring until the gravy thickens and the oil starts to separate. Then add the spices, sugar and salt. Add water if the gravy is too thick.

6. Add the spinach and paneer 2-3 minutes before serving in order to heat through.

7. Remove from heat and stir in cream before serving.

CHETTINAD EGG CURRY

INGREDIENTS

3-5 red chillies (to taste)

2 tsps coriander seeds

½ tsp cumin

¾ tsp fennel seeds

¼ tsp pepper

3 cloves

1 cinnamon stick

2 green cardamom pods

¼ cup (20g, ¾ oz) coconut, chopped or grated

10 cashew nuts

2-3 tbsps oil

1 onion, finely chopped

1 tsp ginger-garlic paste

2 medium tomatoes, cubed, or ½ cup (110g, 4oz) tomato puree

Salt, to taste

4 eggs, boiled and halved

Coriander leaves, chopped, and 1 stem curry leaves, to garnish

METHOD

1. Place a frying pan on a low heat. Add chillies and coriander seeds and dry roast until they turn aromatic, approximately 2 minutes. Then add cumin, fennel, pepper, cloves, cinnamon and cardamom pods. Stir and roast for 1 minute.

2. Turn up the heat to medium. Add coconut and fry for 2 minutes. Next add the cashew nuts and cook for 2 minutes, stirring to ensure they don't burn. Remove from heat and cool for 5 minutes.

3. Grind the nuts and spices in a blender to a fine powder. Add water until a thick paste has formed.

4. Add oil to the frying pan and cook onions until golden, approximately 5-7 minutes. Add the ginger-garlic paste and cook until aromatic, approximately 2 minutes. Add the tomatoes or tomato puree and cook for a further 5 minutes or until the mixture thickens.

5. Add the ground paste and then water as needed to make gravy. Cook on a medium heat until the gravy thickens. Taste and add seasoning if required.

6. To serve place the curry in bowls and top with egg, chopped coriander and curry leaves.

POTATOES WITH MUSTARD SEEDS

INGREDIENTS

3 tbsps vegetable oil or ghee

1 tbsp brown mustard seeds

2 tbsps urad dahl (black lentils)

1-3 dried hot red chillies, halved lengthwise

20 fresh curry leaves

1 onion, chopped

1 tsp salt

½ tsp ground turmeric

½ tsp cayenne pepper

450g (1lb) potatoes, cut into small chunks

1 tomato, chopped

Pinch of ground asafoetida (optional)

1 cup (250ml, 8fl oz) water

METHOD

1. Heat oil or ghee in a large frying pan over medium heat. Add mustard seeds, urad dahl, and chillies. Stir for 20 seconds until the seeds start to pop and the dahl begins to turn red.

2. Stir in curry leaves, if using. Add the onions and fry until soft and golden, approxomately 7 minutes. Add salt, turmeric, and cayenne and stir for 10 seconds. Add potatoes, stir and then fry for 2 minutes.

3. Add the tomato and asafoetida, if using. Fry for 1 minute. Add water and bring to a boil. Cover, reduce heat slightly, and cook until the potatoes are just tender and the water is absorbed. Remove lid and continue to cook for 6-8 minutes, stirring often, until the potatoes are reddish yellow.

PANEER BUTTER CURRY

INGREDIENTS

1 onion, roughly chopped

10 cashew nuts

Small piece ginger, roughly chopped

4 garlic cloves

2 tbsps butter or ghee

1 tsp chilli powder

½ tsp ground cumin

½ tsp garam masala

1 tsp dried fenugreek leaves

2 cups (500ml, 1pt) tomato purée

Salt, to taste

1 tbsp honey

¼ cup (60ml, 2fl oz) milk

¼ cup (60ml, 2fl oz) fresh cream

1 tsp cornflour dissolved with 2 tbsps water

¾ cup (120g, 4oz) frozen peas, cooked

2½ cups (500g, 1lb) paneer, cubed

METHOD

1. Place the onion, cashew nuts, garlic and ginger in a blender and pulse to form a paste. Add a little water if required to blend.

2. Heat the butter or ghee in a large frying pan. Add the prepared paste and cook on medium heat for 1-2 minutes, stirring occasionally.

3. Add the dried spices to the pan with ½ cup (125ml, 4fl oz) of water. Mix well and cook for 1 minute.

4. Add the tomato purée and salt, mix well and cook for a further 2 minutes, stirring occasionally.

5. Add the honey, milk and fresh cream, mix well and cook for 2-3 minutes, stirring occasionally.

6. Add the cornflour and water and stir gently while cooking for 1 minute.

7. Add the peas and paneer, and cook for 1-2 minutes, stirring occasionally. Serve.

SERVES 4 ★ PREP 25MIN ★ COOK TIME 30MIN

MIXED VEGETABLE CURRY

INGREDIENTS

1 tbsp vegetable oil

1 onion, thinly sliced

2 carrots, thinly sliced

2 potatoes, diced

¼ head cauliflower,
cut into florets

½ head broccoli,
cut into florets

1 cup (90g, 3oz)
mushrooms, quartered

½ cup (80g, 3oz)
frozen peas

1 tsp garam masala

2 tsps fennel seeds

¼ tsp ground turmeric

¼ tsp hot chilli powder
(optional)

3 garlic cloves,
finely chopped

Medium piece ginger,
roughly chopped

1 x 400g (14oz) can
chopped tomatoes

5 curry leaves

1 cinnamon stick

Sliced red chilli,
to garnish

METHOD

1. Heat oil in a wok or large frying pan over medium heat. Add onion and fry, stirring occasionally, for 8 minutes or until softened. Next add the potato and cook, stirring occasionally, for a further 5 minutes. Add carrots, cauliflower and broccoli and cook for 2 minutes. Add mushrooms and peas and cook for a further 2 minutes.

2. Add garam masala, fennel seeds, turmeric, chilli (if using), garlic and ginger to the pan. Cook for 2 minutes, stirring gently.

3. Increase the heat to high. Add tomatoes, curry leaves, cinnamon and 1 cup (250ml, 8fl oz) cold water and bring up to a simmer. Reduce heat to low. Simmer, covered, for 10 minutes.

4. Remove lid. Simmer for 10 minutes or until vegetables are tender. Season. Garnish with sliced red chilli and serve.

SERVES 4 ★ PREP 30MIN ★ COOK TIME 20MIN

CAULIFLOWER KOFTA CURRY

INGREDIENTS

1 cauliflower,
cut into florets

½ cup (85g, 3oz) fresh
paneer, grated

4 potatoes,
cooked and mashed

1 tbsp chilli powder

1 tbsp ground coriander

1 tsp ground cumin

1 tsp garam masala

2 tbsps cornflour

Oil, for deep frying

1 tbsp butter

Salt, to taste

1 tsp cumin seeds

2 onions, chopped

1 cup (225g, 8oz)
tomato puree

1 tbsp chilli powder

1 tbsp ground coriander

1 tsp garam masala

Salt, to taste

Boiling water, as needed

¼ cup (60ml, 2fl oz) fresh
cream

Coriander leaves
to garnish

METHOD

1. Place a large pan of salted water on a high heat and bring to the boil. Remove from the heat. Place cauliflower florets in hot water for 5 minutes. Remove and drain.

2. When cool, pat dry and then grate the cauliflower. After 5 minutes, squeeze out excess liquid. Heat a frying pan to a medium-low heat and dry roast the cauliflower for 5 minutes. Set aside to cool.

3. Add the grated paneer, mashed potatoes, ground spices and cornflour to the cauliflower. Mix well. Roll balls of the mixture and place on a plate.

4. Heat oil in a pan on a high heat. When hot, deep fry the koftas until golden brown. When cooked, drain on paper towel to remove excess oil.

5. Heat butter in a pan. Add the cumin seeds and fry for 1 minute. Next add the onions and fry for 5 minutes until soft and translucent. Add the tomato puree and cook for 5 minutes, until thickened.

6. Add the ground spices and salt and stir well. Add water to create the desired consistency and volume of curry sauce. Bring to the boil.

7. Reduce the heat to low and add the cream (reserving a small amount for garnishing). Stir well then add the kofta balls. Simmer on low heat for about 3 to 4 minutes to warm through.

8. Drizzle with cream and garnish with coriander leaves before serving.

DRY CURRIED TOFU

INGREDIENTS

1 block (200g, 7oz) firm tofu, drained and cubed

½ tsp ground turmeric

1 tbsp ground coriander

2 tsps black pepper

1½ tbsps chilli powder

1½ tsps salt

3 tbsps vegetable oil

1 tsp mustard seeds

1 tsp fenugreek seeds

1 large onion, sliced

1½ tsps cumin seeds

5-6 curry leaves

1 tsp garlic paste

2 tsps ginger paste

2 cups (500ml, 1pt) water

1 cup (250ml, 8fl oz) coconut milk

2 tbsps fresh lime juice

METHOD

1. Place tofu in a large bowl, and sprinkle with ground turmeric, ground coriander, black pepper, chilli powder, and salt. Toss the tofu through the spices. Cover bowl, and refrigerate until needed.

2. Heat oil in a large pan over medium heat. Fry mustard seeds, fenugreek, onion, cumin seeds, and curry leaves in oil for about 3-4 minutes. Stir in garlic and ginger pastes, and cook for a further 2 minutes. Add tofu and water, stir, and cover with lid.

3. Bring to a boil, then reduce heat to medium-low and allow to simmer for 20 minutes.

4. Stir in coconut milk, and cook without the lid until almost dry. Stir to keep the tofu from sticking to the bottom of the pan. Stir in lime juice, and serve on a bed of wilted greens.

PEANUT AND SPINACH CURRY

INGREDIENTS

½ tbsp coconut oil

1 onion, chopped

1 tsp garlic, minced

½ cup (90g, 3oz) lentils

1 x 400ml (14fl oz) can coconut milk

2 tbsps coconut cream

¼ cup (65g, 2oz) peanut butter

1 tbsp sugar

1 tsp paprika

1 tbsp fish sauce

Juice of 1 lime

Pinch of chilli flakes (optional)

Pinch of salt

1 bunch fresh spinach, leaves picked

Chopped roasted peanuts, for garnish

METHOD

1. Place the coconut oil in a saucepan over medium heat. Add onion and garlic and cook for 5 minutes or until soft and golden brown

2. Add lentils and coconut milk. Stir and reduce the heat to medium-low. Simmer, uncovered, for 40 minutes until tender.

3. Add coconut cream, peanut butter, sugar, paprika, fish sauce, lime juice, red pepper flakes, if using, and salt, to taste. Stir well and then add spinach. Cover and cook for 1-2 minutes until spinach has wilted.

4. Serve with rice and garnish with chopped roasted peanuts.

JACKFRUIT CURRY

INGREDIENTS

2 cups (320g, 12oz) raw jackfruit flesh, cubed

½ cup (90g, 3oz) cooked chickpeas

6 dried red chillies

¼ tsp mustard seeds

1 cup (90g, 3oz) grated coconut

1 tamarind or ¼ cup (60g, 2oz) tamarind paste

1 tbsp tomato paste

Hot water, as needed

4 small tomatoes, halved

METHOD

1. Bring a large pan of salted water to the boil and cook jackfruit for 10 minutes until tender. Remove from heat, drain and combine with chickpeas. Set aside.

2. Heat oil in a frying pan over medium heat and fry chillies for 2 minutes. Remove and allow to cool then using a pestle and mortar or food processor grind chillis together with mustard seeds, grated coconut, tamarind, tomato paste and salt into a fine paste using water as required.

3. Transfer paste into the pot with jackfruit and stir to combine. Add water to bring the required consistency. Season to taste.

4. Bring curry to the boil, add the tomatoes, and then reduce to a simmer for 5 minutes.

CURRY ROASTED CAULIFLOWER

INGREDIENTS

2 tbsps melted butter or ghee

3 garlic cloves, minced

Medium piece ginger, minced

1 small onion, finely chopped

1 tsp Indian curry powder

Pinch of salt

Ground black pepper

1 small cauliflower, broken into florets

Chopped coriander, to serve

METHOD

1. Preheat the oven to 200°C (400°F, Gas Mark 6). Prepare a baking tray lined with greaseproof paper.

2. Heat a small frying pan over medium-high heat. Add garlic, ginger and onion and fry, stirring, for 10 minutes until sticky and soft.

3. Mix the melted butter or ghee, curry powder, salt and pepper together in a mixing bowl. Add the cauliflower and garlic-ginger mix.

4. Transfer to baking tray arranging in one single layer. Roast for 20 minutes and serve immediately, garnished with chopped coriander.

SERVES 6 ★ PREP 30ᴍɪɴ ★ COOK TIME 15ᴍɪɴ

COCKTAIL SAMOSAS

INGREDIENTS

2 tbsps vegetable oil

1 tsp cumin seeds

½ cinnamon stick

Medium piece ginger, chopped

1 chilli pepper, minced

¼ tsp turmeric

½ tsp garam masala

2 potatoes, diced and parboiled

3 carrots, cooked

1 cup (170g, 6oz) peas, cooked

1 cup (170g, 6oz) corn kernels, cooked

1 tbsp lemon juice

1¼ tsps salt

2 tsps sugar

¾ cup (30g, 1oz) fresh coriander, chopped

2 tbsps flour

Spring roll sheets, thawed

vegetable oil, to deep fry

METHOD

1. In a large pot, heat the oil on medium heat. Add the cumin seeds and cinnamon stick. When the cumin is fragrant, turn the heat to low and add the ginger, chilli pepper, turmeric and garam masala. Stir for 1 minute.

2. Increase the heat to medium and add the potatoes. Stir and cook for 3-4 minutes. Add the rest of the vegetables and cook for a further 3-4 minutes. Stir in the lemon juice, salt and sugar.

3. Remove from the heat and add the chopped coriander. Let the mixture cool. Remove the cinnamon stick.

4. In a small bowl, combine ¼ cup (60ml, 2fl oz) water with the flour and set aside.

5. Cut the spring roll sheets into quarters lengthwise.

6. Take the corner of one strip and fold it to make a cone-shaped pocket. Fill the pocket with a heaped teaspoon of the filling. Fold the strip over to create a triangle shape and seal the remaining edge with a dab of the flour-water mixture.

7. In a large deep-fryer (or frying pan), heat 2cm (1in) vegetable oil to medium heat. To test the temperature, place a small piece of spring roll sheet in the oil. It should sizzle and rise to the top. When ready, fry the samosas in the pan a few at a time, until golden brown, approximately 3 minutes each side.

TOFU, GREEN BEAN AND SPINACH CURRY

INGREDIENTS

2 tbsps olive oil

½ onion, chopped

Medium piece ginger, sliced

1 clove garlic, bruised

1 bay leaf

1 tsp salt

2 tsp mild curry powder

½ tsp ground cumin

²/₃ cup (160ml, 5fl oz) coconut milk

1 cup (170g, 6oz) peas (fresh or frozen)

100g (3½ oz) green beans, trimmed

100g (3½ oz) button mushrooms, quartered

1 x 400g (14oz) package firm tofu, drained and cubed

1 bunch spinach, leaves picked

1 tsp fresh lime juice

Basil leaves, to garnish

METHOD

1. Heat the olive oil in a large saucepan over medium-high heat. Add the onion and fry for approximately 5 minutes or until the onion starts to brown.

2. Next add ginger, garlic, bay leaf and salt. Cook, stirring occasionally, for a further 2-3 minutes. Add the curry powder and cumin and cook, stirring, for 1 minute until aromatic.

3. Increase the heat to high. Add the coconut milk and bring to a boil. Add the peas, beans, mushrooms and tofu and stir.

4. Cover the pot and reduce heat to a simmer, stirring occasionally, until the vegetables are just tender and the tofu is heated through, approximately 3 minutes.

5. Discard the ginger and garlic, stir in the lime juice, and season to taste with salt. Serve on black rice garnished with basil leaves.

SINGAPORE CURRY NOODLE

INGREDIENTS

200g (7oz) rice noodles

6 garlic cloves, chopped

Small piece ginger, chopped

3 red chillies, chopped

2 lemongrass stems, pale part, thinly sliced

1 tsp ground turmeric

5 kaffir lime leaves, finely shredded

2 tbsps coconut oil

4 tofu puffs

2 tbsps sesame oil

3½ cups (875ml, 30fl oz) cups coconut milk

4 cups (1L, 2 pt) vegetable stock

5 baby corn, quartered

5 spring onion, sliced

1 tsp tamarind concentrate

¼ cup (60ml, 2fl oz) soy sauce

1 lime, juiced

Parsley, to garnish

METHOD

1. Soak noodles in a large bowl of hot water for 30 minutes to soften.

2. Meanwhile, place garlic, ginger, chillies, lemongrass, turmeric and kaffir lime leaves in a blender and pulse to form a chunky spice paste.

3. In a large pot over medium heat, stir-fry spice paste in sesame oil for 1-2 minutes until aromatic.

4. Add the coconut milk and vegetable stock and bring to the boil. Next add corn, spring onion and tofu and allow to simmer for 5 minutes. Add tamarind, soy sauce and lime juice. Allow to simmer for another couple of minutes, then remove from heat.

5. Drain noodles and divide among bowls. Pour over the curry sauce and garnish with parsley.

EASY OKRA WITH TOMATOES

INGREDIENTS

Oil, for cooking

½ tsp brown mustard seeds

Pinch of asafoetida

1 onion, thinly sliced

1 clove garlic, finely chopped

¼ tsp cumin seeds

⅛ tsp ground turmeric

1 large tomato, chopped

500g (1lb) sliced okra

¼ tsp chilli powder

1 tsp amchur (dry mango powder)

Salt, to taste

METHOD

1. Heat oil in a frying pan over medium-high heat. Add the mustard seeds and cook until they begin to pop. Mix in asafoetida.

2. Reduce heat to low, and add onion, garlic, cumin seeds and turmeric. Cook, stirring occasionally, for 5 minutes or until onion is soft and golden brown.

3. Add tomato and okra and stir into the mixture. Gradually mix in chilli powder, amchur, and salt. Cook for 15 minutes, stirring occasionally, until okra is tender but firm.

CURRIED CAULIFLOWER FRITTERS

INGREDIENTS

1 head cauliflower
cut into florets

2 tbsps olive oil

4 Asian shallots, chopped

2 tbsps Greek yoghurt

1 lemon, juiced

Salt, to taste

½ cup (60g, 2oz) dry
breadcrumbs

2 eggs

2 tbsps flour

1 garlic clove, grated

1½ tsps curry powder

1 tsp ground cumin

½ tsp turmeric

¼ tsp cinnamon

Vegetable oil for frying

Greek yoghurt and chopped
chives, to garnish

METHOD

1. Preheat oven to 200°C (400°F, Gas Mark 6). Place the cauliflower on a lined baking tray and drizzle with olive oil. Place in the oven for 20 minutes, turning once midway through.

2. Heat oil in a small saucepan on a medium-low heat. Add in the shallots and saute until soft, approximately 6 minutes. Place the cooked shallots, yoghurt, lemon juice and salt in a bowl and stir to combine. Set aside.

3. Transfer the cauliflower to a food processor and pulse until the mixture is coarsely ground. Place the cauliflower in a large bowl and add the shallot mix along with breadcrumbs, eggs, flour, spices and salt. Mix thoroughly until combined. Cover the bowl and transfer to the fridge to chill for 3 hours.

4. Take spoonfuls of the mixture and use your hands to form the patties. Repeat until all mixture has been used up.

5. Place a frying pan over medium-high heat, and pour in vegetable oil until it reaches 1cm (½in) up the sides. Add the fritters, cooking 2 or 3 at once. Cook for 2-3 minutes until golden brown. Gently flip and cook on the opposite side for 1-2 minutes. Transfer to paper towels to drain. Repeat to cook the rest of the fritters.

6. Serve with a dollop of Greek yoghurt and garnish with chopped chives.

BROCCOLI, CASHEW NUT AND KALE CURRY

INGREDIENTS

⅓ cup (40g, 1½oz) toasted cashew nuts

1 cup (250ml, 8fl oz) water

1 tbsp coriander seeds

2 tsps cumin seeds

1 cinnamon stick

3 cloves

2 tbsps coconut oil

1 tsp salt

1 tsp turmeric powder

1 head broccoli, broken into florets

1 small head cauliflower, broken into florets

METHOD

1. Place cashews and water in a blender and pulse on high for 30 seconds. Set aside.

2. Heat a large frying pan over medium heat. Add coriander, cumin, cinnamon stick and cloves and dry fry until seeds start to brown and are fragrant. Cool and then pound spices in a pestle and mortar or grind in a spice grinder.

3. Add turmeric, broccoli and cauliflower and continue to sauté for 2-3 minutes.

4. Reduce heat to low and stir in the cashew liquid. Bring to a gentle simmer and continue to cook for 5 minutes until vegetables are tender.

SPICY SALAD OF CURRIED RICE BALLS

INGREDIENTS

Vegetable oil, for
deep-frying

1 cup (200g, 7oz) cold
cooked long grain rice

1 cup (90g, 3oz)
unsweetened
desiccated coconut

½ tsp salt

1½ tbsps Thai red
curry paste

1 tbsp cornflour

¾ cup (90g, 3oz) rice
flour (or plain flour)

Cold water

230-340g (8-12oz) naem

Fish sauce, to taste

Fresh lime juice, to taste

Dried chilli flakes,
to taste

6 spring onions, chopped

¾ cup (15g, ¾ oz) coriander
leaves, and dried chillies,
to garnish

METHOD

1. Heat the vegetable oil in a large frying pan over a medium-high heat. Make sure the oil is at least 8cm (3in) deep.

2. Meanwhile mix the rice, coconut, salt, curry paste and cornflour together and roll into balls.

3. Mix the rice flour with a few tablespoons of cold water to make a thin batter.

4. Test the oil by dropping in a tiny bit of batter. It should sizzle and bubble to the surface. When hot enough, dip the rice balls into the batter and drop them into the hot oil. They should float to the surface quickly. Separate with a spoon to keep them from sticking together.

5. Lower the heat to medium-high and fry the rice balls for 20-30 minutes, turning to ensure even browning. When cooked, remove with a slotted spoon and rest on paper towels until cool.

6. To make the salad, crumble the naem in a large salad bowl. Add the cooled rice balls to the bowl and crumble them up with your hands. Add chopped green onions. Season with fish sauce and lime juice to taste. Add red pepper flakes to taste.

7. Serve the salad garnished with coriander and chillies.

SERVES 6 ★ PREP 15MIN

CURRIED EGGS

INGREDIENTS

12 eggs, hard boiled
and cooled

1½ tsps curry powder

2 tbsps mayonnaise

1 tsp salt

Ground paprika and
chopped fresh dill,
to garnish

METHOD

1. Peel the eggs and halve lengthways.

2. Scoop out yolks and place in a bowl.

3. Add curry powder, mayonnaise and salt to yolks.
   Mash with a fork and combine.

4. Spoon the mixture into the halved egg whites.

5. Sprinkle lightly with paprika and garnish with
   chopped dill.

POTATO AND PEA CURRY

INGREDIENTS

2 tsps brown mustard seeds

2 tbsps ghee or vegetable oil

2 onions, chopped

2 garlic cloves, crushed

2 tsps fresh ginger, minced

1 tsp ground turmeric

½ tsp chilli powder

1 tsp ground cumin

1 tsp garam masala

750g (1½lb) plain potatoes, diced

Salt and pepper, to taste

1 cup (170g, 6oz) frozen peas

Sprig of mint, to garnish

METHOD

1. Heat a large saucepan over medium-high heat. Add mustard seeds and cook until they start to pop. Add the oil or ghee, onion, garlic and ginger and fry over medium heat for 5 minutes, or until the onion is soft.

2. Add the turmeric, chilli powder, cumin, garam marsala and potato and cook for 1-2 minutes, stirring to coat the potato with the spices. Taste and season with salt and pepper.

3. Add ½ cup (125ml, 4fl oz) water and bring to the boil. Reduce the heat to medium-low, cover and simmer for 15-20 minutes, or until the potato is just tender.

4. Stir in the peas, then cover and simmer for 3-5 minutes, or until the potato is cooked and the liquid is absorbed. Season more if needed and serve, garnished with mint.

SERVES 20 ★ PREP 30MIN ★ COOK TIME 30MIN

EASY CURRY PUFFS

INGREDIENTS

2 tbsps peanut oil

1 onion, finely chopped

½ tsp ginger, grated

1 clove garlic, crushed

2 potatoes, peeled and finely diced

½ small sweet potato, peeled and finely diced

1 small eggplant, finely chopped

3 tbsps Thai red curry paste

¾ cup (120g, 4oz) frozen peas

1 tbsp kecap manis

1 tsp fish sauce

5 butter puff pastry sheets, thawed

1 egg, lightly beaten

METHOD

1. Preheat the oven to 200°C (390°F, Gas Mark 6) and prepare a baking tray with greaseproof paper.

2. Heat oil in a saucepan or wok over a medium-low heat. Cook onion, ginger and garlic for 2 minutes until soft.

3. Add potatoes, eggplant, curry paste, peas, kecap manis and fish sauce. Cook for 7-8 minutes until potato is tender although not fully cooked.

4. Cut circles from the pastry sheet using a cookie cutter. Place a tablespoon of mixture on one half of each circle leaving room around the edges. Fold the circle over to form a semi-circle and them roll the edge and squeeze to seal.

5. Place on baking tray and brush lightly with egg. Cook in oven for 20 minutes until brown. Serve warm.

OKRA MASALA CURRY

INGREDIENTS

Oil for frying

250g (9oz) okra, topped and tailed

1 onion, chopped

1 tsp ginger-garlic paste

2 tomatoes, chopped

1 tsp ground coriander

½ tsp red chilli powder

½ tsp ground turmeric

½ tsp garam masala

½ tsp amchur (dry mango powder)

Salt, to taste

METHOD

1. Rinse the okra in water and then leave to dry or wipe with a kitchen towel.

2. Heat 2 tablespoons of oil in wok or large frying pan. Add okra and cook, stirring frequently, until tender and no longer crunchy, approximately 5-7 minutes. Set aside.

3. Heat 1 tablespoon of oil on a medium-high heat and add the onions. Fry for 5 minutes, until translucent. Add the ginger-garlic paste and saute for 1 minute until aromatic.

4. Add the chopped tomatoes and saute until soft. If the tomato mixture becomes too dry add water and continue cooking.

5. Add the dry spice powders, stir well and saute for 1 minute.

6. Add the okra and mix so that the onion-tomato masala coats the okra well. Taste and season with salt as needed. Cook for a further 2-3 minutes and then serve.

JAMAICAN PUMPKIN AND PINEAPPLE CURRY

INGREDIENTS

4 garlic cloves, chopped

3 spring onions, chopped

Large piece ginger, chopped

1 tbsp lime juice

2 sweet potatoes, chopped

225g (½lb) pumpkin, cubed

Salt and pepper, to taste

1½ tsp dried thyme

1-2 tbsps coconut oil

1 cup (160g, 6oz) sweet pineapple, cubed

2 bay leaves

1 cup (250ml, 8fl oz) coconut milk

½ tsp ground allspice

Sesame seeds and mint, to garnish

METHOD

1. Place garlic, green onions, ginger and lime in a blender or food processor and blend to create a curry paste.

2. Put the sweet potato and pumpkin into a large bowl. Sprinkle over salt and thyme and rub into the vegetables. Cover with the curry paste and toss to coat. Cover and set aside to marinate for 2 hours.

3. Preheat the oven to 180°C (350°F, Gas Mark 4).

4. Heat the coconut oil in a large frying pan on a medium heat. Add the sweet potato and pumpkin and fry for 1 minute. Then reduce the heat to low, cover the pan and cook for 5 minutes.

5. Add the pineapple with a dash of black pepper, stir, re-cover and cook for a further 5 minutes. Add the bay leaves, coconut milk and allspice and stir to combine.

6. Transfer the curry from the pan into an oven-proof casserole dish and place in the oven for 1 hour.

7. Serve on white rice, garnished with sesame seeds and a sprig of mint.

SIMPLE POTATO CURRY

INGREDIENTS

Curry paste

½ onion, coarsely chopped

2-3 garlic cloves

1 green chilli

1 tsp red chilli powder

½ tsp ground turmeric

½ tbsp ground coriander

Curry

2 tbsps oil or ghee

½ onion, finely chopped

½ tsp cumin seeds

3-4 potatoes,
cut into chunks

2 tomatoes, roughly
chopped

Salt, to taste

½ tsp garam masala

1¼ cups (310ml, 10fl oz)
water

½ cup (10g, ½ oz) coriander
leaves, chopped

METHOD

1. Place coarsely chopped onion, garlic, green and red chillies, turmeric and coriander into a blender, add water and pulse to make fine paste. Set the curry paste aside.

2. Heat oil or ghee in a saucepan and when hot add the cumin seeds. Let the seeds pop and then add finely chopped onion. Fry until the onion becomes translucent, approximately 7-10 minutes.

3. Add curry paste to the pan and fry until the paste just starts to separate from the oil. Then add the potato, stir and cover. Allow potato to cook on a low heat for 2 minutes.

4. Next add the tomato and salt, stir and cook for 2-3 min over a low heat. Add 1¼ cups (310ml, 10fl oz) of water to the pan. Turn up the heat and boil for 1 minute then again reduce to a simmer and cover the pot.

5. When potatoes are cooked soft, approximately 10 minutes, add garam masala and coriander leaves and stir.

SWEET PINEAPPLE CURRY

INGREDIENTS

Oil, for frying

1 onion, sliced

2 green capsicum seeded and sliced

½ tsp black mustard seeds

Small piece ginger, grated

2 garlic cloves, crushed

455g (1lb) can pineapple chunks, drained and juice retained

1½ tsps curry powder

¼ tsp turmeric

1 tsp fish sauce

6 curry leaves

1 tbsp sugar

¼ cup (60ml, 2fl oz) coconut milk

Dried red chillies and curry leaves, to garnish

METHOD

1. Heat the oil in a large saucepaon over medium-high heat. Add onion and green capsicum and fry for 3 minutes or until just soft and slightly golden. Add mustard seeds and fry for 1 minute until they just start to pop. Add ginger and garlic and fry for 1-2 minutes until aromatic.

2. Add pineapple, curry powder, turmeric, fish sauce and curry leaves. Stir well to blend and coat pineapple with the spices. Cook, stirring, for 3 minutes.

3. Add half of the pineapple juice to the pan and cook for 2 minutes. Add more pineapple juice to achieve the desired consistency.

4. Add sugar and coconut milk and simmer for 2 minutes.

5. Serve garnished with chillies and curry leaves.

MANGO CURRY

INGREDIENTS

1 cup (250ml, 8fl oz) coconut milk

3 ripe mangoes, peeled and diced

2 dried red chillies

1½ tsps mustard seeds

1 tsp vegetable oil

1 sprig curry leaves

¼ tsp turmeric

Pinch of asafoetida or hing powder (optional)

2 tsp grated jaggery or sugar

Salt, to taste

METHOD

1. Place coconut milk, ½ cup (115g, 4oz) of mango flesh, chillies and ½ tsp mustard seeds in a blender or food processor and pulse until combined into a rough curry paste. Set aside.

2. Heat the oil in a deep-sided frying pan over a medium-high heat and add the remaining mustard seeds. Cook, stirring, for 1 minute until the seeds start to pop, and then add curry leaves, turmeric and asafoetida or hing, if using.

3. Add the remaning mango and curry paste. Add a cup (250ml, 8fl oz) of water or more to achieve the desired consistency, and stir in the jaggery or sugar. Add salt to taste.

4. Heat until the curry just simmers. Remove from the heat and serve with rice.

EASY PALAK PANEER

INGREDIENTS

900g (2lb) spinach

Salt, to taste

2-3 green chillies

3 tbsps oil

½ tsp cumin seeds

4-6 garlic cloves,
finely chopped

225g (8oz, ½ lb) paneer,
cubed

1 tbsp lemon juice

4 tbsps fresh cream

METHOD

1. Remove stems and wash spinach thoroughly in running water. Blanch in salted boiling water for 2 minutes. Refresh in chilled water. Squeeze out excess water.

2. Place spinach and green chillies in a blender or food processor and grind into a fine paste.

3. Heat oil in a frying pan on a meduim heat. Add the cumin seeds. When they begin to darken, add garlic and saute for half a minute. Add the spinach puree and stir.Check seasoning.

4. Add water if required. When the gravy comes to a boil, add the paneer and mix well. Stir in lemon juice.

5. Before serving stir in fresh cream. Serve hot with naan bread.

TOMATO EGGPLANT CURRY WITH MILLET

INGREDIENTS

1 large eggplant, diced

1 tsp salt

2 tbsps ghee (or butter)

1 cup (200g, 7oz) hulled millet

2 cups (500ml, 1pt) cold water

Knob of butter

3 cloves garlic, finely chopped

Small piece ginger

1 tsp ground cumin

1 tsp ground coriander

½ tsp ground turmeric

Pinch of ground cinnamon

3 tomatoes, finely diced

Lemon juice, to taste

Coriander leaves, chopped, to garnish

METHOD

1. Place eggplant in a large bowl, sprinkle over the salt and stir to combine. Set aside for 20-30 minutes.

2. Heat the ghee in a saucepan over medium-high heat. Add millet and fry, stirring often, for a minute or so, until toasted. Add cold water and a pinch of salt and bring to the boil. Reduce heat to low and cover. Cook for 20 minutes. Remove from the heat and set aside for 5 minutes before adding a knob of butter and fluffing with a fork

3. Pat eggplant dry using a paper towel. Heat ghee in a large frying pan over medium heat. Add the eggplant and cook for 5 minutes, stirring often until golden and starting to soften. Add the garlic and ginger and cook for 1 minute, stirring constantly. Add spices and cook for 1 minute until fragrant. Add chopped tomatoes and a dash of water to prevent sticking.

4. Reduce heat to a low simmer and cover. Cook for 10 minutes until the eggplant is soft and tomato has formed a thick gravy. Season to taste with salt and lemon juice.

5. Serve curry with millet, garnished with coriander leaves.

SPICY JAPANESE TOFU WITH ENOKI MUSHROOMS

INGREDIENTS

1 pkt silken tofu, cubed

1 tbsp cornflour

1 cup (250ml, 8fl oz) dashi

½ cup (75g, 3oz) kimchi

100g (3½ oz) enoki mushrooms

½ tsp gochujang (available at Asian supermarkets)

Spring onion, sliced, to garnish

METHOD

1. Pat the tofu dry with a paper towel. Cut into cubes and rest on a paper towel. Place a tray or chopping board on top and weigh down with a bowl. Leave to rest for 15 minutes. Toss the dry tofu in cornflour.

2. Meanwhile, fill a deep pan a third full of oil, and heat to about 180°C (350°F), or until it sizzles on frying.

3. Drop tofu into the oil and cook until crisp and golden, turning with tongs, approximately 2 minutes each side. When cooked, scoop out and drain on paper towel.

4. Place dashi, kimchi, enoki mushrooms, tofu and gochujang in small pot. Cook on medium heat until hot, about 6-7 minutes. Reduce heat to low. Cover pot and cook another 3 minutes.

5. Dress plate with some of the sauce and add fried tofu and enoki mushrooms on top. Drizzle with extra sauce. Garnish with spring onion and serve.

CRISPY POTATO BHAJIAS

INGREDIENTS

3 potatoes, finely grated

1 tsp salt, for soaking

3 tbsps fresh coriander, chopped

2 green chillies, chopped

1 red chilli, chopped

1 garlic clove, minced

1 cup (95g, 3oz) besan (gram or chickpea flour)

½ tsp salt

1 tsp chilli powder

¼ tsp pepper

Pinch of ground turmeric

1 tsp cumin seeds

1 tsp ajwain (carom seeds) (substitute cumin or caroway seeds)

Pinch of bicarbonate of soda

Oil, for frying

METHOD

1. Rinse potato under the tap and then drain. Place in a bowl of salted water and soak for 15 minutes. Drain the potato from the salty water and rinse once more. Drain.

2. Place drained potatoes in a bowl and mix through the coriander, chilli sand garlic.

3. In the meantime, mix all the dry ingredients except the bicarb together.

4. On a large plate, sprinkle some of the dry ingredients, and then place some potato mix on top. Repeat this layering of dry ingredients and potato mix until all ingredients have been used. Set aside and rest for 30 minutes. (The potatoes will release moisture to hold the bhajia together.)

5. When ready to fry, add a pinch of bicarb to the potatoes then bring the mixture together with your hands.

6. Heat oil in a large frying pan on medium heat and deep fry for 5 minutes or until potatoes are properly cooked and the bhajias are browned and crispy. Cook in batches if needed.

BREAD, CONDIMENTS AND RICE

Sri Lankan roti   222
Fish biryani   224
Easy naan   226
Raita   228
Garlic naan   229
Butter roti   230
Fresh tomato chutney   231
Indian lime pickle   232
Coconut rice with curry leaves   234
Rice crepes   236
Chicken biryani   238
Crispy fried onions   239
Mango chutney   240
Balinese sambal   241
Mushroom pilau rice   242
Mint coriander sauce   244
Curry powder   246
Pappadams   247
Saffron rice with grilled capsicum   248
Tomato sambal   250
Red curry paste   252
Green curry paste   253

SRI LANKAN ROTI

INGREDIENTS

1 cup (90g, 3oz) freshly grated coconut or desiccated coconut

Salt, to taste

3 cups (375g, 12oz) plain flour, sifted

1 cup (250ml, 8fl oz) cold water

1 tbsp vegetable oil

1 onion, finely chopped

¼ cup (25g, 1oz) finely chopped chillies

Olive oil, for frying

METHOD

1. Soak the desiccated coconut for 20 minutes.

2. Combine the salt, coconut and vegetable oil with the flour and mix well. Gradually add the water, a little at a time until it forms a dough, not too soft but a dry and workable dough.

3. Heat the olive oil in a small frying pan. Fry the onion on a medium heat for 5 minutes or until soft. Combine with the chillies and gently combine with the dough.

4. Roll the dough into balls. Use a piece of lightly greased silver foil to flatten the dough ball into a round shape.

5. Heat olive oil in a heavy-duty frying pan on medium-high heat. Cook on both sides well browned, approximately 3 minutes each side. Cook in batches.

FISH BIRYANI

INGREDIENTS

1 tsp chilli powder

¼ tsp ground turmeric

½ tsp ground fennel

½ tsp salt

500g (1lb) white fish,
cut into chunks

2 cups (310g, 8oz)
basmati rice

2 onions

3 cloves garlic

Medium piece ginger

¼ cup (5g, ¼ oz) mint

2 tbsps ghee (or butter)

1 cinnamon stick

4 cloves

4 cardamom pods

4 Asian shallots, chopped

1 tsp chilli powder

½ tsp ground turmeric

1 tsp ground fennel

½ tsp garam masala

¼ cup (40g, 1½oz) sultanas

Crispy fried onions and
fresh mint, to garnish

METHOD

1. Combine chilli, turmeric, fennel and salt and rub spices into fish. Cover and place in refrigerator until ready to use.

2. Rinse rice 3 times and then soak in water for 20 minutes.

3. Place onions, garlic, ginger and mint leaves in food processor and process to create a paste.

4. Heat ghee in a frying pan over medium-high heat. Add paste and fry for 5 minutes. Remove and set aside.

5. In the same pan fry the marinated fish pieces for 5 minutes until golden, turning half way through. Remove and set aside.

6. In a separate pan, cover the rice with water and cook for 12 minutes.

7. Meanwhile, add cinnamon stick, cloves and cardamom to the frying pan and cook for 1-2 minutes. Add in shallots and fry for 1 minute. Add the onion paste and fry until fragrant. Add chilli, turmeric, fennel and garam masala.

8. Drain the basmati and mix with the masala. Add sultanas and mix through. Add fish pieces and gently combine.

9. Serve with crispy fried onions and sprig of mint, to garnish.

EASY NAAN

INGREDIENTS

1½ cups (185g, 6oz) self-raising flour

²/₃ cup (160ml, 5fl oz) warm water

1 tbsp ghee or vegetable oil

1 tsp salt

50g (2oz) unsalted butter, melted

1 tsp poppy or sesame seeds (optional)

METHOD

1. Place the flour in a large mixing bowl and add the water, ghee or oil, and salt and mix together well. Add some extra water or flour as required for a workable dough.

2. Knead for 3-5 minutes on a floured working surface until you have a smooth dough.

3. Place the dough back in the bowl, cover, and leave in a warm place to rise for 1½ hours.

4. Preheat grill for 10 minutes until very hot. Grease an oven plate.

5. Knead the risen dough for 2 minutes and divide into 4-6 equal portions. Roll out to a thickness of about 1cm (½in).

6. Place the dough on oven plate and grill for 7-10 minutes, turning once or twice. Each time, brush the surface of the bread with some butter and, if using, sprinkle poppy or seseame seeds over the bread.

INDIAN RAITA

INGREDIENTS

½ cup (125ml, 4fl oz) plain yoghurt

½ cucumber, seeded and chopped

2 tbsps fresh coriander, chopped

2 tsps spring onions, finely chopped

¼ tsp ground coriander

¼ tsp ground cumin

Pinch of cayenne pepper and fresh mint, to garnish

METHOD

1. Mix all ingredients in medium bowl. Season to taste with salt.

2. Chill, covered, until ready to serve.

3. Garnish with cayenne pepper and fresh mint.

GARLIC NAAN

INGREDIENTS

1½ tsps dry active yeast

¾ cup (185ml, 6fl oz) warm water

2 tsps sugar

1½ cups (185g, 6oz) whole wheat flour

1½ cups (185g, 6oz) plain flour

2 tsps garlic, minced

1½ lemon juice

1 tsp salt

4 tbsps oil or ghee

2 tbsps garlic, finely chopped

1-2 tbsps chopped celery leaves or coriander leaves (optional)

1 tsp nigella seeds

Oil or ghee, for frying

METHOD

1. Place yeast, warm water and sugar in a small bowl. When bubbling, add flours, garlic paste, lemon juice, salt and oil to the mixture.

2. Knead to a smooth dough, adding water if required. Cover with a moist cloth and allow to leaven for 1-2 hours. When dough has doubled in size, roll into medium-sized balls. Cover and set aside for 15-20 minutes.

3. Mix garlic, celery leaves and nigella seeds together on a plate.

4. Knead the risen dough for 2 minutes and divide into 4-6 equal portions. Roll out to a thickness of about 1cm (½in). Place this disc into the garlic-celery-nigella-seeds mixture.

5. Heat oil or ghee in a frying pan. Place the naan garlic-side-down in the hot pan. Cook until charred then flip and cook the reverse until charred.

BUTTER ROTI

INGREDIENTS

2 cups (250g, 8oz) flour

1 tsp salt

2 tbsps melted butter

²/₃ cup (160ml, 5fl oz) water

1 tbsp olive oil

METHOD

1. In a large bowl, sift together flour and salt. Add butter and combine with a fork until mixture is crumbly. Gradually add the water until the dough pulls together.

2. Turn dough out onto a floured surface and knead until smooth and elastic, about 8 minutes. Cover and set aside for 45 minutes.

3. Knead dough again until smooth. Divide into 8 equal parts and form into rounds. Roll out each round as thinly as possible. Keep dusting with flour as needed to prevent sticking.

4. Place a heavy cast-iron pan upside down over burner and heat. Spread roti over base of pan and cook. Roti will cook in 40 to 50 seconds.

FRESH TOMATO CHUTNEY

INGREDIENTS

1 tbsp ghee

6 curry leaves

½ tsp mustard seeds

½ tsp chilli flakes

5 large tomatoes, chopped

¼ tsp ground turmeric

1 cinnamon stick

1 tbsp caster sugar

2 tbsps sultanas

1 tsp ginger, grated

¹/₃ cup (80ml, 3fl oz) water

METHOD

1. Heat the ghee in a medium frying pan over medium-low heat.

2. Add the curry leaves, mustard seeds and chilli to the pan. Cook, shaking the pan, for 1 minute or until the seeds start to pop.

3. Add the tomatoes and turmeric. Cook, stirring, for 1 minute.

4. Add the cinnamon, sugar, sultanas, ginger and water.

5. Increase heat to high and bring to the boil. Reduce the heat to low and simmer for 10 minutes, stirring occasionally, until the chutney is thick.

6. Allow to cool before serving

INDIAN LIME PICKLE

INGREDIENTS

1kg (2lb) limes

¹/₃ cup (90g, 3oz) salt

40 garlic cloves, crushed

50g (2oz) red chilli powder

²/₃ cup (150ml, 5fl oz) vegetable oil

3 tbsps black mustard seeds

3 tbsps white cumin seeds

½ tsp asafoetida

METHOD

1. Cut each lime into eight pieces. Place the limes in a bowl and add the salt, garlic cloves and red chilli powder. Mix well coating the limes fully. Place in a bowl, cover and marinate in the fridge for 4 hours. Retain any juices and place in a separate container in the fridge.

2. Place limes in steamer and steam for about 15 minutes until they are quite soft.

3. Transfer the lime mixture to a glass bowl and cover with a towel. Leave in a warm place for 2 days to marinate further, stirring twice a day to re-coat the limes.

4. At the end of day 2, heat the vegetable oil in a frying pan over medium-high heat. When the oil is hot, add the black mustard seeds, cumin seeds and asafoetida. When mustard seeds begin to pop, remove from the heat. Pour the oil over the limes and stir well.

5. Retrieve lime juices from fridge and pour over limes.

6. Cover again with the towel and allow to sit in a warm place for another 2 days.

7. Scoop the lime pickle into a food processor and process to a chunky paste.

8. Place in a sterilised airtight container and let sit in a cool place for at least 2 weeks before serving.

COCONUT RICE WITH CURRY LEAVES

INGREDIENTS

1 tbsp sunflower oil

1 tbsp mustard seeds

1 cup (155g, 4oz) basmati rice, rinsed 3 times

¼ cup (45g, 2oz) chickpeas (cooked)

2 cups (500ml, 1pt) coconut milk

20 curry leaves

Large pinch of salt

METHOD

1. Heat the oil in a saucepan on medium heat. Add the mustard seeds. When they start to pop, add in the basmati rice. Stir a little to coat the rice with the oil and to distribute the mustard seeds evenly. Add chickpeas and stir.

2. Add in the coconut milk, 15 curry leaves and salt. Bring to a boil and then cover with a lid and turn down the heat to a simmer. The rice should be cooked in 12-15 minutes.

3. Fluff up and serve with the rest of the fresh curry leaves as a garnish.

RICE CREPES

INGREDIENTS

2 eggs

2 cups (160g, 6oz) rice flour

2 cups (500ml, 1 pt) milk

Olive oil, for frying

METHOD

1. Mix together the eggs, flour and milk with a fork until a smooth batter forms.

2. Heat a frying pan and pour ½ tablespoon oil in it.

3. When the oil is smoking pour a ladle of batter into one point in the pan and then roll pan from side to side to allow the batter to spread evenly.

4. Cook for 1-2 minutes. Check the underside and when it is done to the desired colour, flip and cook the second side for a further 1-2 minutes.

5. Repeat the same steps with new oil each time until you finish all the batter.

6. Serve immediately.

CHICKEN BIRYANI

INGREDIENTS

300g (10oz) three-colour pilau rice

25g (1oz) butter or ghee

1 onion, finely sliced

1 bay leaf

3 cardamom pods

1 cinnamon stick

1 tsp ground turmeric

4 skinless chicken breasts, cut into 1cm (½ in) chunks

½ cup (80g, 3oz) raisins or sultanas

3½ cups (875ml, 30fl oz) chicken stock

Chopped coriander and crispy fried onions, to garnish

METHOD

1. Soak the rice in warm water, then rinse in cold until the water runs clear.

2. Heat the butter or ghee in a saucepan and fry the onions with the bay leaf and other whole spices for 10 mins. Sprinkle in the turmeric, then add chicken and pan-fry until aromatic.

3. Add the rice and raisins or sultanas to the pan and stir for 1 minute before pouring in the stock. Put a tight-fitting lid on the pan and bring to a boil. Lower the heat to the minimum setting and cook for another 5 mins.

4. Remove from the heat and leave to stand with the lid on for 10 mins. Stir well, mixing through half the coriander.

5. To serve, scatter over the rest of the coriander and the crispy fried onions.

CRISPY FRIED ONIONS

INGREDIENTS

4 large onions, thinly sliced

½ cup (125ml, 4fl oz)
vegetable oil for deep frying

METHOD

1. Heat the oil on medium-high in a wok or deep frying pan.

2. Add the onions in two batches, frying each batch for 6-8
   minutes until golden brown. Stir constantly so that onions are
   evenly fried. Do not allow the onions to blacken and burn.

3. Remove from pan with a slotted spoon and drain on paper
   towel. Leave for 10 minutes to dry out and crunch up.

4. Store leftovers in an airtight container.

PREP 5MIN ★ COOK TIME 1HR

MANGO CHUTNEY

INGREDIENTS

1½ kg (3lb 5oz) mangoes, diced

2 large red chillies, de-seeded and chopped

Medium piece ginger, finely grated

1 lemon, juiced and zested

2 cups (500ml, 1pt) white wine or cider vinegar

750g (1½lb) brown sugar

1 tsp cumin powder

1 tbsp salt

2 cloves garlic, crushed

1 tsp allspice powder

1 tsp turmeric (optional)

METHOD

1. Place all ingredients in a large heavy-based pot and bring to the boil, stirring often.

2. Reduce heat and cook for 1 hour or until mixture is thick.

3. Bottle and seal.

BALINESE SAMBAL

INGREDIENTS

1 tsp shrimp paste

100g (3½ oz) Asian shallots, thinly sliced

1 small orange capsicum, diced

10 pieces lemongrass, thinly sliced

2 limes, juiced

2 red chillies, thinly sliced

2 tbsps peanut oil

METHOD

1. Heat a frying pan on a medium heat and roast the shrimp paste for 2 to 3 minutes.

2. In a bowl, mash the roasted shrimp paste with all the other ingredients until a smooth paste forms.

3. Taste and add more chilli if required.

MUSHROOM PILAU RICE

INGREDIENTS

1 cup (200g, 7oz) basmati rice

6 tbsps vegetable oil

6 green cardamom pods

2 cinnamon sticks

10 cloves

2 bay leaves

2 spring onions, sliced

1-2 red chillis, sliced

125g (4oz) white mushrooms, sliced

2 cloves garlic, finely chopped

½ tsp salt

2 cups (500ml, 1pt) water

Small pinch of saffron

METHOD

1. Rinse the rice in cold water until the water runs clear.

2. Heat half the oil in a large pan and add the cardamom pods, cinnamon sticks, cloves and bay leaves and stir for 1 minute.

3. Add the spring onion and chilli and cook for 1-2 minutes, followed by the mushrooms and garlic and fry for a further 10 minutes.

4. Add the rice and salt and stir until the rice is well coated in the oil. Pour in the water and bring to the boil.

5. After 4-5 minutes much of the water will have evapourated. Stir in the saffron strands, cover and reduce the heat to the lowest possible setting for 12-15 minutes, or until the rice is tender.

MINT CORIANDER SAUCE

INGREDIENTS

1 bunch mint

2 bunches fresh coriander

2 tsps green chillies, chopped

8 spinach leaves

1 tsp chopped ginger

1½ tbsps lemon juice

¾ tsp roasted cumin seeds

10 almonds

½ tsp salt

¼ tsp asafoetida

1 tsp sugar

²/₃ cup (160ml, 5fl oz) water

METHOD

1. Remove mint leaves from stems.

2. Remove hard and thick stems from coriander. Chop leaves and soft stems.

3. Place all the ingredients in a spice grinder or pestle and mortar and grind to make a smooth paste. Add water while grinding.

4. Remove and store in an airtight jar for up to 2 weeks.

PREP 5MIN
CURRY POWDER

INGREDIENTS

2 tbsps cumin seeds,
toasted

2 tbsps cardamom pods,
toasted

2 tbsps coriander seeds,
toasted

¼ cup (45g, 2oz)
ground turmeric

1 tbsp dry mustard

1 tsp cayenne

METHOD

1. Place all ingredients in a glass container with an airtight lid and shake to combine.

2. Store in a cool dry place for up to 6 months.

3. When ready to use, place required amount in a spice grinder or pestle and mortar and grind to a fine powder. Add to dishes according to taste.

MAKES 12 ★ PREP 20MIN ★ COOK TIME 2HR 5MIN

PAPPADAMS

INGREDIENTS

4 cups (380g, 13oz)
lentil flour

1 tsp pepper

½ tsp ground cumin

1 tsp cumin seeds

½ tsp salt

¼ cup (60ml, 2fl oz) water

Vegetable oil, for frying

METHOD

1. Preheat the oven to 100°C (210°F, Gas Mark ¼) and lightly oil 3
    baking trays.

2. Combine flour, black pepper, ground cumin, cumin seeds and
    salt in a large bowl.

3. Bring the dough together by hand until smooth, gradually
    adding water to achieve a firm and moist dough that is not too
    sticky.

4. Divide dough into 12 balls and roll out each ball on a slightly
    oiled surface to a very thin round layer.

5. Place onto baking tray and put the pappadams in the oven for 2
    hours until dried out. Remove and store in an airtight container
    until ready to serve.

6. When ready to eat, heat oil in a frying pan over a high heat
    until shimmering. Drop the pappadams in one by one and fry
    for a minute until the edges begin to fold. Do not brown. Serve
    immediately.

SAFFRON RICE WITH GRILLED CAPSICUM

INGREDIENTS

½ red capsicum, finely diced

½ yellow capsicum, finely diced

1 onion, finely chopped

2 tbsps olive oil

2 garlic cloves, finely chopped

1 cup (200g, 7oz) long grain rice

Salt, to taste

2 cups (500ml, 1pt) water

½ tsp ground saffron or pinch of saffron threads

1 tbsp oyster sauce (optional)

1 tsp sesame oil

¼ cup (10g, ¼ oz) chopped parsely

Parsely leaves, to garnish

METHOD

1. Preheat grill. Grill capsicums until blackened on all sides. Transfer to a bowl and cover with plastic wrap. Leave for 15 minutes. Peel and cut into bite-size pieces.

2. Heat oil in a medium saucepan with a tight-fitting lid over medium heat. Add onion and garlic and cook, stirring, for 5 minutes, until soft. Add rice and salt; stir to coat.

3. Add 2 cups (500ml, 1pt) water and saffron to the pot. Bring to a boil and then reduce heat to low. Cover and cook for 40–45 minutes, until all liquid is absorbed. Remove from heat and leave covered for 5 minutes, and then remove lid and fluff rice with a fork.

4. Transfer rice to a large serving bowl and season to taste with salt and pepper. Stir in grilled capsicum. Add oyster sauce if using and and mix well. Stir through chopped parsely and garnish with parsley leaves.

TOMATO SAMBAL

INGREDIENTS

4 long red chillies, seeded

5 small bird's-eye chillies

4 Asian shallots

6 garlic cloves

4 tomatoes, roughly chopped

1 tbsp palm sugar

1 tsp shrimp paste

4 candlenuts

1/3 cup (80ml, 3fl oz) oil

Salt, to taste

METHOD

1. Put the chillies, shallots, garlic, tomatoes, palm sugar, shrimp paste, candlenuts and salt in a food processor and pulse until the mixture is thick and resembles a tomato salsa.

2. Heat the oil in a wok or large frying pan over medium heat. Fry the tomato mixture for 5-10 minutes, until it reduces by nearly half and the oil rises to the surface.

3. If the sambal is dry, add more oil. Season to taste.

RED CURRY PASTE

INGREDIENTS

1 shallot, roughly chopped

1 stalk lemongrass, pale part, roughly chopped

1-2 red chillies

4 cloves garlic, peeled

1 large piece galangal or ginger, roughly chopped

2 tbsps tomato puree

1 tsp ground cumin

¾ tsp ground coriander

¼ tsp white pepper

2 tbsps fish sauce

1 tsp shrimp paste

1 tsp sugar

1½ tbsp chilli powder

3 tbsps thick coconut milk

2 tbsps lime juice

¼ tsp ground cinnamon

METHOD

1. Place all ingredients in a food processor, blender or pestle and mortar and process well to create a fragrant Thai red curry paste.

Notes:

To thin down the sauce, add a little more coconut milk.

Paste will taste very strong at this point, but will mellow when curry ingredients are added.

Store in an airtight container in the fridge for up to 2 weeks.

PREP 10MIN

GREEN CURRY PASTE

INGREDIENTS

½ tsp coriander seeds

¼ tsp cumin seeds

6 white peppercorns

1 tsp shrimp paste

¼ tsp ground turmeric

4 coriander roots,
roughly chopped

2 lemongrass stems
(white part only), roughly
chopped

1 tbsp galangal or ginger,
grated

1 long green chilli,
roughly chopped

4 small green chillies,
roughly chopped

4 kaffir lime leaves,
roughly chopped

2 Asian shallots,
roughly chopped

4 garlic cloves,
roughly chopped

METHOD

1. Toast coriander and cumin seeds with the peppercorns in a
   wok or frying pan over medium heat for 1-2 minutes until
   fragrant, stiring to prevent burning.

2. Cool slightly. Grind to a fine powder using a mortar and pestle
   or spice grinder.

3. Dry-fry shrimp paste in a wok or pan over medium heat for 1
   minute to toast slightly.

4. Cool, then add to mortar or grinder with all the remaining
   ingredients and pound with pestle until roughly crushed.

5. Add 1 tablespoon water and use a stick blender (or transfer
   to a food processor) to blend to a paste.

Notes:

Store in an airtight container in the fridge for up to 2 weeks.

INDEX

anchovies
  nasi lemak 118
apple
  lamb and apple curry pita 92
beef
  beef curry benedict 71
  beef kofta in tomato sauce 63
  beef massaman curry 68
  beef rendang 80
  coconut beef curry 72
  curried meatball sandwich 66
  Jamaican jerk patty 74
  Japanese curry rice with cheese
    and fried egg 102
  Kerala fried beef 79
  meatballs in curry sauce 76
  pad kee mao drunken noodle 86
  simple beef samosa 62
  slow beef madras 64
  South African bobotie 82
  spiced beef stew with
    pomegranate 88
  Vietnamese beef pho 104
broccoli
  broccoli, cashew nut and kale
    curry 196
  mixed vegetable curry 179
  pad kee mao drunken noodle 84
capsicum
  curried prawn kebabs 115
  pad kee mao drunken noodle 84
  saffron rice with grilled
    capsicum 248
cashews
  broccoli, cashew nut and kale
    curry 196
  cashew and red bean curry 152
cauliflower
  cauliflower kofta curry 180
  curried cauliflower fritters 194
  curry roasted cauliflower 187
  mixed vegetable curry 179
cheese, See also paneer
  Japanese curry rice with cheese
    and fried egg 102
chicken
  balti chicken 43
  best butter chicken 22
  Bombay chicken wings 42
  Burmese curry noodles 20
  charred tandoori drumsticks 44

chicken and potato curry 49
chicken biryani 238
chicken coconut curry 13
chicken haleem 34
chicken jalfrezi 50
chicken laksa 38
chicken malvani 26
chicken massaman curry 25
chicken noodle khao soi 54
chicken tikka masala 32
chicken tikka wrap 18
chicken vindaloo 19
classic chicken curry 36
curried chicken salad 31
doro wat (Ethiopian curry) 52
easy red chicken curry 8
easy tandoori chicken 48
green chicken curry 46
hot Japanese ramen 10
jerk chicken 14
Korean fire chicken 30
spicy chicken breast 12
spicy Korean chicken 16
spicy okra and chicken
  gumbo 40
sweet chicken curry pie 37
tandoori chicken kebabs with
  chapatti and salad 28
chickpeas
  black chickpea curry 169
  chickpea channa masala 150
  chickpea spinach curry 149
  roasted spicy chickpeas 148
cinnamon
  green cinnamon lentils 142
clams
  hot fried clams 114
coconut
  beef rendang 80
  chicken coconut curry 13
  coconut beef curry 72
  coconut rice with curry leaves 234
coriander
  mint coriander sauce 244
cucumber
  raita 228
curry powder 246
duck
  sweet duck red curry 24
eggplant
  curried chicken salad 31

easy curry puffs 203
pork, eggplant and red lentil
  curry 101
tomato eggplant curry with
  millet 214
eggs
  Chettinad egg curry 174
  curried eggs 200
  Japanese curry rice with cheese
    and fried egg 102
fish
  classic fish curry 110
  easy yellow fish curry 134
  fish biryani 224
  Indonesian spicy snapper 129
  Kerala fish curry 132
  Penang laksa 136
  steamed fish with curry paste 135
  Thai fish curry bowl 112
  tomato and sardine curry 120
  Vietnamese spicy fish 126
  whole fish with yellow curry 130
green curry
  green chicken curry 46
  green curry paste 253
jackfruit
  jackfruit curry 186
jerk
  Jamaican jerk patty 74
  jerk chicken 14
  spicy okra and chicken
    gumbo 40
kale
  broccoli, cashew nut and kale
    curry 196
kidney beans
  cashew and red bean curry 152
  kidney bean curry 154
  South African bean curry 155
lamb
  bunny chow 70
  easy crockpot lamb and pumpkin
    curry 87
  lamb and apple curry pita 92
  lamb rogan josh 58
  Moroccan curry meatballs 90
  South African bobotie 82
  spiced lamb chops 94
lentils
  chicken haleem 34
  chilli lentil soup 146

classic yellow dahl 166
curried lentil patties 158
dahl tadka 163
green cinnamon lentils 142
green lentil curry 162
lentil and potato crepes 164
pork, eggplant and red lentil
    curry 101
red lentil Indian soup 156
spinach and lentil soup 168
traditional dahl makhani 160
lime
Indian lime pickle 232
mango
mango chutney 240
mango curry 211
millet
spicy vegan curry burgers 144
tomato eggplant curry with
    millet 214
mint
mint coriander sauce 244
mushrooms
mixed vegetable curry 179
mushroom pilau rice 242
spicy Japanese tofu with enoki
    mushrooms 216
mutton
mutton and tomato curry 78
noodles
Burmese curry noodles 20
chicken laksa 38
chicken noodle khao soi 54
easy prawn laksa 138
hot Japanese ramen 10
pad kee mao drunken noodle 84
Penang laksa 136
Singapore curry noodle 192
spicy Korean chicken 16
Thai fish curry bowl 112
Vietnamese beef pho 104
okra
easy okra with tomatoes 193
okra masala curry 204
spicy okra and chicken gumbo 40
onion
crispy fried onions 239
paneer
easy palak paneer 212
paneer butter curry 178
prawn and paneer curry 122

spinach paneer butter
    masala 172
pappadams 247
peanuts
chicken massaman curry 25
nasi lemak 118
peanut and spinach curry 184
peas
mixed vegetable curry 179
paneer butter curry 178
potato and pea curry 202
pineapple
Jamaican pumpkin and pineapple
    curry 206
sweet duck red curry 24
sweet pineapple curry 210
pomegranate
spiced beef stew with
    pomegranate 88
pork
Jamaican pumpkin and pork
    curry 98
pork, eggplant and red lentil
    curry 101
pork Penang 96
pork tonkatsu 60
simple pork curry 93
spicy mapo tofu 106
Thai-style pork curry 84
potato
chicken and potato curry 49
cocktail samosas 188
crispy potato bhajias 218
lentil and potato crepes 164
mixed vegetable curry 179
potato and pea curry 202
potatoes with mustard seeds 176
simple potato curry 208
prawns
BBQ chilli lime prawns 121
creamy tom yum kung 116
curried prawn kebabs 115
easy prawn laksa 138
prawn and paneer curry 122
prawn curry fried rice 124
spicy stir-fried prawns 128
pumpkin
easy crockpot lamb and pumpkin
    curry 87
Jamaican pumpkin and pineapple
    curry 206

Jamaican pumpkin and pork
    curry 98
raita 228
ramen
hot Japanese ramen 10
red curry
easy red chicken curry 8
red curry paste 252
sweet duck red curry 24
Thai fish curry bowl 112
saffron
mushroom pilau rice 242
saffron rice with grilled
    capsicum 248
sardines
tomato and sardine curry 120
sausages
curry wurst with French fries 100
spinach
chickpea spinach curry 149
easy palak paneer 212
peanut and spinach curry 184
spinach and lentil soup 168
spinach paneer butter masala 172
tofu, green bean and spinach
    curry 190
sweet potato
curried lentil patties 158
easy crockpot lamb and pumpkin
    curry 87
easy curry puffs 203
Jamaican pumpkin and pineapple
    curry 206
spicy vegan curry burgers 144
tofu
dry curried tofu 182
Singapore curry noodle 192
spicy Japanese tofu with enoki
    mushrooms 216
spicy mapo tofu 106
tofu, green bean and spinach
    curry 190
tomato
easy okra with tomatoes 193
fresh tomato chutney 231
tomato eggplant curry with
    millet 214
tomato sambal 250
yellow curry
easy yellow fish curry 134
whole fish with yellow curry 130

First Published in 2016 by Herron Book Distributors Pty Ltd
14 Manton St
Morningside
QLD 4170
www.herronbooks.com

Custom book production by Captain Honey Pty Ltd
PO Box 155
Byron Bay
NSW 2481
www.captainhoney.com.au

Cataloguing-in-Publication. A catalogue record for this book is available from the National Library of Australia

ISBN 978-0-947163-05-1

Printed and bound in China by Shenzhen Jinhao Color Printing Co., Ltd

5 4 3   17 18 19 20

NOTES FOR THE READER

Preparation, cooking times and serving sizes vary according to the skill, agility and appetite of the cook and should be used as a guide only.

All reasonable efforts have been made to ensure the accuracy of the content in this book. Information in this book is not intended as a substitute for medical advice. The author and publisher cannot and do not accept any legal duty of care or responsibility in relation to the content in this book, and disclaim any liabilities relating to its use.

PHOTO CREDITS

Front cover: Nataliya Arzamasova
Back cover: Joshua Resnick
Aimee M Lee p 41. AJP p 120. AleksandraN p 183. Alphonsine Sabine p 73, 81, 219, 223, 228, 245. Andrey Starostin p 115, 229. Anna Shepulova p 148. Anna_Pustynnikova p 157. AS. Food studio p 17, 19, 25, 65, 69. Bernd Juergens p 27. Brent Hofacker p 201, carlosdelacalle p 13. CGissemann p 231. D-Stocker p 186. David Wingate p 105. Daxiao Productions p 177. Digivic p 77. Dogolbayeva Nadezhda p 37. Dolly MJ p 36, 119, 251. Ekaterina Kondratova p 162. Elena Veselova p 179, 197. espies p 205, 230. Eva Gruendemann p 155. Eve's Food Photography p 163, 167, 209, 235. FatManPhoto p 233. Gelladilemma p 31. grass-lifeisgood p 137. Hans Geel p 92. highviews p 62. hlphoto p 111, 134. inewsfoto p 131. Jamesbox p 127. Jamie Rogers p 247. JAZZDOG p 24. Joe Gough p 18, 29. Joshua Resnick p 15, 173. Josie Grant p 149. Jyothi Rajesh p 175, 181. Kelvin Wong p 107. Kentaro Foto p 128. ktasimar p 252. KYTan p 39. Lapina Maria p 165. lenisecalleja.photography p 83. Lesya Dolyuk p 99. Mahathir Mohd Yasin p 239. manzrussali p 192. margouillat photo p 9. Martin Turzak p 43, 51, 101, 125. Mateusz Gzik p 121. Matthew Oldfield p 129. Maxene Huiyu p 217. Monkey Business Images p 123. Mukesh Kumar p 154, 161. Natalia Klenova p 56, 108. Nataliya Arzamasova p 143, 153, 185, 215, 240, 249. nattanan726 p 114. norikko p 48. Odua Images p 59, 241. Olha Afanasieva p 246. Onizu3d p 135. onkey Business Images p 243. Ozgur Coskun p 227. Paul_Brighton p 30, 53, 70, 75, 78, 87. Peiling Lee p 49. PI p 210. PiggingFoto p 117. Piotr Krzeslak p 193, 207. Piyato p 55, 61. qanatstudio p 93. Radu Dumitrescu p 139. Ramon grosso dolarea p 45, 147. SAHACHATZ p 199. Santhosh Varghese p 79, 211. sashi p 100. seeshooteatrepeat p 238. Shaiith p 33, 151. Simon Booth p 140. SOMMAI p 97. Stasis Photo p 95. Stepanek Photography p 23, 67, 195. stockcreations p 91 suriya yapin p 47. svry p 42. Tatiana Bralnina p 11. tavizta p 85. Thanthima Lim p 203.Thidarii p 103. Tomophafan p 253. travellight p 63. Ulyana Khorunzha p 191. VICUSCHKA p 1, 2, 6., 56, 108, 170, 220 vm2002 p 35, 133, 159, 168, 169, 178, 187, 189, 202, 213, 225, 237. Vorontsova Anastasiia p 12. walkdragon p 21. WEERACHAT p 113. Yuliya Gontar p 2, 170, 220.
Images used under license from Shutterstock.com
p 89, 100, 145 © bigstockphoto.com